OTHER BOOKS BY PHILIP KRILL

Ursprung

Intuitions from God-knows-where

PHILIP KRILL

authorHOUSE®

AuthorHouse™
1663 Liberty Drive
Bloomington, IN 47403
www.authorhouse.com
Phone: 833-262-8899

Published by AuthorHouse 06/20/2024

ISBN: 979-8-8230-2831-8 (sc)
ISBN: 979-8-8230-2832-5 (e)

Editorial Assistance: Jessica Livengood

Print information available on the last page.

This book is printed on acid-free paper.

For

Barbara Ann Krill
September 15, 1951 - June 6, 1952

"The wind blows where it wills, and you hear the sound of it, but you do not know where it comes from or where it goes; so it is with every one who is born of the Spirit."

John 3:8

CONTENTS

INTRODUCTION

Both the inspiration and title for this book appeared unbidden last summer (2023) on a bright, balmy morning in Interlaken, Switzerland. It was as if God were saying to me: 'You needn't have traveled to the Alps to find the beauty you seek; look, rather, into your heart'. All of what is written here comes from that epiphanic *Ursprung* of intuition.

If brain-storming is an exercise in mental imagination, *Ursprung* is an example of soul-storming. Unlike brainstorming, the aphorisms that comprise *Ursprung* arise from a *Source* (*Ursprung*) more 'beyond and above' the ideas that brainstorming produces. This book is a collection of such inspirations, originally unconnected but gradually formed into sections and chapters which I hope exhibit a natural, organic affinity. I wrote *Ursprung* more as an act of obedience than originality. This book offers a vision of deification, springing from contemplative prayer, that I believe both the church and the world needs. The reader can be the judge.

I dedicate this book to my sister, Barbara Ann Krill. Barbara lived but 9 months, yet has ever since been my intercessor before the throne of God. In some measure, I do what I do and write what I write because of her vigilant love and prayers.

6 June 2024
Feast of (my) St. Barbara

Ursprung (German) - Source, Origin

PART ONE

TRINITAS

Archē

God's apparent absence from the world is God's way of being present to the world. God is a Divine Mystery of ever-receding yet ever-present Uncreated Light and Love.

God is *that with which* the eye sees and the ear hears. As Meister Eckhart says, 'The eye ('I') with which I see God is the same eye ('I') with which God sees me'.[1]

The Light of God transcends the human intellect. The light of our understanding is made possible by, but is altogether 'other' than, the Uncreated Light of God.

'In God's light we see light' (cf. Ps. 36:9). God's uncreated Act of Being (*Actus Purus*) 'precedes', and makes possible, all created forms of creation. Grasping this 'real distinction'[2] is itself a divine intuition coming from God-knows-where.

---

[1] '*The eye through which we see God is the same eye through which God sees us; our eye and God's eye are one eye, one seeing, one knowing, one love*' (Meister Eckhart, *Sermon IV*, 'True Hearing'.
[2] The so-called 'real distinction' refers to the distinctive relation between the Creator and the creation. In his work, *On Being and Essence*, St. Thomas Aquinas introduces his account of the real distinction between *esse* (existence) and *essentia* (essence). In both immaterial and material substances, Aquinas thinks, we find a real distinction

A 'golden thread of analogy' saves us from 'the contagion of equivocity'[3] when speaking of God. Because of the Incarnation, all that can be predicated of human beings can also be predicated of God, albeit in a pre-eminent way.

God is 'ever-greater' than anything that can be accurately said of God.[4] Anagogy saves analogy from being equivocity. Analogy saves anagogy from disappearing into an apophatic abyss.

Those who abide in the 'analogical interval' made possible by an anagogical vision of the Incarnation are filled with continuous gratitude. They experience a delight and a joy the world cannot give.

---

and composition of esse and *essentia*; only in God are these principles identical. This distinction is not easily grasped in its deepest meaning, however. For this, see: Daniel Soars, *The World and God are Not-Two: A Hindu-Christian Conversation*, where he draws on the writings of David Burrell, Kathryn Tanner, Denys Turner and Robert Sokolowski to bring to light the absolute incommensurability of our grammar about God and our grammar about the world.

[3] On the 'contagion of equvoicity', see David Bentley Hart, *That All Shall Be Saved: Heaven, Hell and Universal Salvation*, 74-88.

[4] The 'Ever-Greater' is a term used by the mystic Adrianne von Speyr to connote the the anagogical and dynamic fullness of the triune God in all His interactions with us. See her book, *The Boundless God*.

God's is a why-less Love.[5] God does as God is. Creation *ex nihilo* is creation *ex Deo* - a cosmic, finite extension of God's own Life as that which is not God.

Nothing that is not *of God. In God*, all things live and move and have their being (cf. Acts 17:28).

'Being loved' and 'existing' are the same thing in God. Once 'God' is apprehended as *Actus Purus* (Pure Act), we intuit our own naturally divine humanity.

God is no-thing of which we can conceive. God is the ineffable, inexhaustible, unimaginable Pure Act (*Actus Purus*) of Divine Love in which all things receive their *'is-ing-ness'*.

'God' is an ineffable *Actus Purus* of luminous Darkness from which Uncreated Light eternally proceeds. 'God' is the incomprehensible Mystery of unknowable Nothingness, creating, sustaining, and superseding all that is made.

---

[5] A phrase common in the writings of Meister Eckhart. See: Paul E. Szarmach, *An Introduction to the Medieval Mystics of Europe*, 253.

In the heart of the Trinity, the distinction between 'natural' and 'supernatural' disappears. If we have the eyes to see, creatureliness itself is an extension of, and participation in, God as *Actus Purus*.

Because God is as a trinitarian Mystery of pure Love, it is somehow 'natural' - almost 'necessary' - for God to pour Himself out in the act of creation. Must there not be a sense in which, because of *how God is within Himself* that God cannot *not* create?

Imagining 'grace' as something added to 'nature' for its sanctification is like giving a fish a glass a water to satisfy its thirst.

There is no such thing as 'pure nature' existing prior to the gift of 'grace'. All 'two-tiered schemes' of nature and grace are ontologically nonsensical, given the unconditionally gracious self-expression of God as *Actus Purus*.

Creation is intrinsically hard-wired to God. Creation is 'graced' 'all-the-way down'.

God is sophianically present in all that God has made.

There is nothing in us that is not of God. Our existence is a participation in God as the great I AM (cf. Ex. 3:14).

Creation *ex nihilo* stands as a perpetually sustained miracle of Divine Love. Creation is the finite expression of God as *Actus Purus*.

Creation is not an afterthought of God. God did not 'decide' to create. He *cannot not* create because he *is* the Creator.

God does as God is, and God is as God does. Freedom and necessity are lovingly one in God.

Finite existence is frozen grace. The world, as we know it, is solid love. Matter and energy are interchangeable extensions of God's unconditioned beneficence.

Grace is to nature as God is to creation. This relation is so infinitely asymmetrical as to require a grammar we do not possess.[6]

---

[6] As David Burrell has pointed out, the way in which we articulate the *the relation of God to the world* and the nature of God's *distinctiveness from the world* governs and shapes, not simply the rest of our talk about God. If we fail to express how God is 'Other' from the world *in a properly transcendent way*, we fall prey to a pantheistic

'Grace' is not a 'substance' given by God as our commodity Grace is God's self-communication wherein God gives himself for the divinization of all God has made.

God is to the world as negative space is to art. God is the ever-receding, un-thematic Background of all possible created foregrounds.

The world's 'otherness' from God is itself a sacrament of God's intra-trinitarian self-divestment, and an affirmation of the world's intrinsic goodness.

Our creation unto deification is reason God extends himself beyond himself without the loss of himself. We are conceived in, from, and for God in Christ (cf. Col. 1:16).

We are not simply beneficiaries of God's love; we are finite begettings *of* God's Love. We are begotten *by* God for participative union *with* God (cf. 1 Jn. 5:18).

---

identification of creation with the Creator. If, on the other hand, we fail to express properly how God relates to the world *in a non-competitive way*, we will imagine God and the world as two realities of similar ontological weight existing in parallel to each other. See David Burrell, *Creation and the God of Abraham and Freedom* and *Creation in Three Traditions*.

Creation is 'other' from God in a manner analogous to the way in which Father, Son and Spirit are 'other' from each other. Just as the Father is in the Son and the Son is in the Father, so is God in the world and the world is in God without either confusion or conflation.

The world is *in* God (cf. Acts 17:28) and God is *in* the world, yet the world is not God and God is not the world. This is because the 'communion and otherness'[7] which characterizes the life of the Trinity is the template (*tropos*)[8] for the relation of creation to its Creator.

God's 'real distinction'[9] from the world is identical with God's logical relation with the world. This is the contemplative depth of the axiom that 'the economic Trinity is the immanent Trinity'.[10]

---

[7] See the works of John D. Zizioulas, *Being as Communion: Studies in Personhood and the Church* and *Communion and Otherness: Further Studies in Personhood and the Church*.

[8] ***Tropos*** (Greek: τροπη) means 'the way in which' or the 'manner with which' one thing is related to (or oriented towards) another.

[9] See above, n. 1.

[10] A Rule put forward by Karl Rahner reads: 'The economic Trinity is the immanent Trinity'. See Karl Rahner, *The Trinity*. See also, Fred R. Sanders, *The Image of the Immanent Trinity: Rahner's Rule and the Theological Interpretation of Scripture*.

We *are* because God *is*. Until we grasp the radical distinction between the miracle of existence ('*that* anything is') and essence ('*what* anything is'),[11] the Mystery of God as *Actus Purus* remains unknown and unknowable.

The ontological distinction between the Creator and his creation finds its origin in the trinitarian relations. The *Ur-kenosis*[12] of the Trinity is the Source and template for God's relation to the world.

'Absolute difference' and 'inseparable union' are divine excellences both in God and in the world.

---

[11] Experiencing the fundamental difference between existence (*esse*) and essence (*essentia*) is known as 'the intuition of being'. The 'intuition of being' distinguishes between *what* a thing is (its 'nature' or 'essence') from the fact *that* it is (i.e., its own 'act of existing'). It is a grasp of '*the act of existing*' - a perception that is direct and immediate, superior to any discursive reasoning or demonstration a reality which it touches and which takes hold of it.

[12] *Ur-kenosis* - a German term, indicating an original or earliest form of something. *Ur-kenosis* means the original or first instance of 'self-emptying'. Hans Urs von Balthasar speaks of three 'cascading *kenoses*', flowing, as it were, from the Original or *Ur-kenosis* beginning with the Father in the Trinity: '[A] first *kenosis* of the Father, expropriating himself by generating' the consubstantial Son. Almost automatically, this first *kenosis* expands to a *kenosis* involving the whole Trinity. For the Son could not be consubstantial with the Father except by self-expropriation; and their We, that is, the Spirit, must also be God if he is to be the 'personal seal of that self-expropriation that is identical in Father and Son...This primal *kenosis* makes possible all other kenotic movements of God into the world; they are simply its consequence'. *Theo-Dramatics, IV*, 331.

The world comes from God and is, at every moment, desired, willed and held together in God (cf. Col. 1:17). How could anything or anyone ever be separated from the loving *Actus Purus* of its own existence?

At every instant, the whole of creation 'participates'[13] in God as its ineffable *Ür-grund* (Source). And if in its Creator, so also in its Redeemer. Creation itself *is* salvation, anagogically conceived.

God is the Pure Act (*Actus Purus*) from which all things are created, and Christ is God's *Logos* in whom all things hold together (cf. Col. 1:17). The 'laws of nature' participate in the *Logos* of God.

'My ways are not your ways, says the Lord. As high as the heavens are above the earth, so high are my ways above your ways' (cf. Isa. 55:8-9). The *Logos* (logic) of God is completely other from that which governs our sinful world.

---

[13] For a meticulous study of the philosophical and theological uses of 'participation', see Andrew Davison, *Participation in God*.

Awe-filled humility is the only appropriate posture for those who know God as the *Actus Purus* of existence. Hyperbolic stammering is the best we can do when alluding to the experience of 'God'.

God's apparent absence from the world reflects God's ineffability. As *Actus Purus,* God can only be apprehended, never comprehended.

Contemplative prayer is the God-given way to know the unknowable God. 'Be still, and know that I am God' (cf. Ps. 46:10; Mt. 6:6-7).

The transcendent intimacy with which God is present to his creation is apprehended, not with philosophical sophistication, but with intentionally and persistently entering the Cloud of Unknowing.[14]

Orienting ourselves toward God as the great 'I know not what' is the essence of prayer. Our desire for God *is* knowledge of God, since God is the transcendental *Source* of our desire for God.

---

[14] *The Cloud of Unknowing* is an anonymous 14th century English mystical tract outlining an apophatic path to God.

Aphorism, hyperbole and exaggeration seem especially fitting ways to say what we might about God who is 'Ever-greater' than our conceptions of God.[15]

The only knowledge of God available to us is that of the incredulous. The moment the *thought* of 'God' becomes manageable, we consign ourselves to an epistemological hell.

Purity of heart is a by-product of experiencing God as Pure Act (*Actus Purus*). When we apprehend God as the Why-less Source of ever-exceeding Beneficence, we are flooded with a participative share in God's Uncreated Light and Love.

Our minds can never get to the bottom of themselves, just as we can never catch our shadows. Awareness of our unrestricted desire to know is itself a kind of *knowing* that transports us beyond cognition.

Awareness of our capacity for awareness is a participation in God's trinitarian self-awareness. Our intuition of God as the Source of our unrestricted desire to know brings us a share of God's divine joy.

---

[15] In his *Proslogion*, St. Anselm (11th century) referred to 'God' as 'that of which nothing greater can be conceived'. Similarly, the mystic's experience of God is that of an 'Ever-greater God' who is forever beyond all boundaries and comprehension. See Matthew Lewis Sutton, *The trinitarian Mysticism of Adrienne von Speyr.*

What is prayer? Contemplative prayer is abiding in the analogical interval between the world we know and the unknowable God.

We feel an unexpected ecstasy when we surrender our attempts to grasp the unknowable God. Dwelling in the darkness of 'learned ignorance', we apprehend a Light the darkness can neither comprehend nor conquer (cf. Jn. 1:5).

A-theism is essential to genuine faith. A-theism is a prophetic acid that dissolves every idea of God that substitutes for the *experience* of God.

Atheism delivers us from our ideational idols. It cleanses the temples of our minds so that the true God may manifest his Presence in the holy of holies of our hearts.

Atheism is a practical impossibility. Every denial of God's existence is a tacit desire for absolute Truth, which is God.

In formally rejecting God, the atheists assert something they believe to be true. Every such claim of truth presupposes an unthematic horizon of Absolute Truth, which is God. Put simply: God is the Source of the atheist's inspiration to deny the existence of God.

Desire of any kind is an intrinsic yearning for the Absolute, i.e., something that is absolutely good, beautiful and true. Such is the meaning of 'God', transcendentally understood.

God calls himself, 'I AM' or 'I AM who I AM' (cf. Ex. 3:14). Such is God's way of saying: 'I AM beyond naming, beyond description, beyond adjectival identification'.

If God is 'I AM', who are we? We are 'they who *are*' *in* the One who is 'I AM'.

That which inspires us to seek is *That* for which we are seeking.[16] God is always closer to us than we are to ourselves.[17]

---

[16] '*Tat Tvam Asi*' ('You are That') - a text from the Upanishads iindicating the co-inherent unity of *Brahmin* (God) with *Atman* (soul) in every human person.

[17] A paraphrase of St. Augustine's famous phrase, '*Interior intimo meo et superior summo meo*' ('higher than my highest and more inward than my innermost self') (*Confessions* III, 6, 11).

Enter the Cloud of Unknowing.[18] There, transfigured by the Uncreated Light of God, we acquire the countenance of Moses, resplendent with a radiance unknown on earth (cf. Ex. 34:30-33).

'God' is as good a word - or as worthless a word - for That which is beyond words. Any surrogate for 'God' - say, 'Divine Mystery' - is invariably objectified, thereby defeating its purpose as pointing towards the Infinite.

Even the word, 'Infinite' is wanting in its ability to connote the ineffable Mystery called 'God'. The reification of 'God' is the suicide of theology.

C. S. Lewis once remarked that the person in search of God is like the mouse in search of the cat. That for which we seek is seeking us.[19]

The experience of God always has something *arresting* about it. If, when contemplating God, we do not experience *Sacchidānanda*,[20] something is missing.

---

[18] See above, n. 14.

[19] A paraphrase of Mevlana Rumi's famous phrase, 'What you seek is seeking you'.

[20] *Sacchidānanda is* a Hindu term that connotes the divine Bliss (*Ananda*) that arises within us when our Awareness (*Chit*) rests in Being (*Sat*), not in thinking.

Nothing about God is not surprising to our usual ways of perception. By embracing our *ignorance* about God, the 'Light from on high dawns upon us' (cf. Lk. 1:78).

More vain than the fish's search for water is our search for God.

The desire for solitude is a common, and tacit, desire for God. Solitude is a call to be alone with the Alone. Loneliness is a summons from God to find our togetherness in him.

'That for which you seek is seeking you' (Rumi). 'The kingdom of God is within you' (Jesus). 'You are that' (*Upanishads*). Could there be any better confluence of expressions about the Presence of God?

It is because God is a self-diffusive Mystery of Divine Mercy that we 'who need of mercy were created, so that God who is Mercy would not exist in vain'.[21]

God is not the opposite of anything, thus believers have no argument to pick with anyone.

---

[21] St. Irenaeus: 'Since he who saves (Christ himself) always existed (in the Trinity), it was necessary that those who need to be saved (us) should be created, so that he who saves should not exist in vain'. (*Against Heresies*, 3.22.3, quoted in John Behr, *The Mystery of Christ: Life in Death*, 77.)

Logos

Scandal (*skandalon*) is an essential and unchanging component of our experience of God. Awareness of God always 'scandalizes' our normal understanding.

'Blessed is the one who finds no stumbling block (scandal/*skandalon*) in me' (cf. Lk. 7:23). The gospel of Christ scandalizes the logic of sinful humanity.

The Uncreated Light of Christ flashes through the fissures in our mimetic[22] insanity once we run out of energy to 'keep up with the Jones'. It's only when we *doubt* our ability to compete in the rat race that the ray of Christian hope alights.

Pretense is the default posture of a world whose only peace is founded on the threat of violence. 'Might makes right' cannot possibly be true, except in a world where truth is held hostage by bribery and blackmail.

---

[22] Borrowed from René Girard's famous 'mimetic theory'. 'Mimetic' means 'imitative'. For an introduction to mimetic theory, see: https://www.youtube.com/watch?v=5Qu6vBebwwg.

The impact of Incarnation of the Christ is an *Apocalypse* (unveiling, revelation) which the world cannot comprehend. Christ 'turns the tables' (cf. Jn. 2:15) on any religion or politics that promotes 'the myth of redemptive violence'.[23]

The scandalous and redemptive singularity of the Christian *kerygma*[24] for culture and history is lost on those deceived by the wisdom of the world. Such 'wisdom' is 'foolishness to God' (cf. 1 Cor. 3:19).

The influence of Christ has permeated culture everywhere, yet remains largely unknown, even to many of those professing the name Christian. Unbelievers often grasp the scandal of the gospel better than believers themselves.[25]

Christianity is the *end of religion* as the objectification of God and the legitimation of sinful social arrangements.[26] Christ replaces ritualistic religion with a sacramentally synergistic relationship with God that stands athwart the norms of public respectability.

---

[23] A phrase made famous by Walter Wink, https://www2.goshen.edu/~joannab/women/wink99.pdf.

[24] **Kerygma** – Greek word meaning message or announcement. It is used in the New Testament to refer to the act of preaching, and in time was used to refer to the preached message about salvation.

[25] See Pope Benedict XVI's analysis of Jewish scholar Jacob Neusner's critique of Christianity in his book, *Gospel, Catechesis, Catechism: Sidelights on the Catechism of the Catholic Church*, 64-72.

[26] See Buxy Cavey, *The End of Religion*.

The gospel of Christ is a two-edged sword (cf. Heb. 4:12). It slices through the illusions of politicians and religionists alike, affording a different vision of the utopia they seek.

The cross of Christ stands as an eternal sign of what the world thinks of the ways of God. Deicide is humanity's default position.

The cosmos-redeeming miracle of the Incarnation remains a *skandalon* which neither the world nor the institutional church has yet to grasp. 2,000 years removed from the actual event, we are still in the days of the early church.

The meteoric impact of Christ on the world has yet to be fully felt. For a world and a church blinded by notions of retributive justice, St. Paul's vision of all things reconciled in Christ (cf. Jn. 12:32; 1 Cor. 15:24-28) still seems a pipe dream.

The 'disarming of the powers and principalities' which Christ accomplished remains largely hidden beneath the continuing, ever-escalating reciprocal violence that is the foundation of human culture from the beginning.[27] Yet, the gospel of Christ is the 'mystery hidden for ages and generations but now made manifest to the saints' (cf. Col. 1:26; Eph. 3:9; 1 Cor. 2:7).

---

[27] See René Girard, *Things Hidden Since the Foundation of the World*.

21

Secularists seeking to mitigate political conflicts are unaware of the source of their own endeavors, which is Christ. Political correctness is a by-product of the gospel.

The demise of Christendom is the doing of Christ himself. Christ has dissolved every barrier separating peoples, de-legitimizing every form of heteronomy, including Christianity itself (cf. Gal. 3:28; Col. 3:11).

The de-Christianization of western culture is a result of the *kerygma*.[28] Christ has abolished the distinction between sacred and secular, revealing violence as the world's sacred ritual for salvation.[29]

By 'disarming the powers and principalities of the world' (cf. Col. 2:15), Christ has opened a Pandora's box of unimaginable horrors. Dissolving every barrier separating 'us' from 'them' (i.e., 'good guys' vs. 'bad guys'), Christ has created the conditions for apocalyptic violence.

---

[28] See above, n. 24.
[29] See René Girard, *Violence and the Sacred*.

By destroying the social ramparts which, by their power of segregation and slavery, create and maintain a modicum of worldly peace, Christ has opened the way to mass destruction. Christ's disavowal of violence has given *carte blanche* for violence to those unconverted by the Spirit.

Christ's disarmament of the demons has unchained Satan for an apocalyptic reign of terror (cf. Rev. 20:7). Christ has shown the emperors of this world to have no clothes, and now they seek their revenge.

The agony of Christ began long before he sweated blood in the Garden (cf. Lk. 22:44). It began when, before the foundation of the world, Christ saw that the whole of humanity, predestined to be holy and blameless in his sight (cf. Eph. 1:4), had exchanged its divine birthright for a bowl of the world's violent gruel (cf. Gen. 25:29-34).

Compelled by divine pity, Christ left the company of his Father and, in the fullness of time, came to rescue a deceived and disenfranchised humanity. Christ came to save us from our attempts to eliminate violence by employing violence.

Christ affords a peace 'the world cannot give' (cf. Jn. 14:27). The world underwrites peace by perpetuating war; Christ offers peace by disarming evil with self-sacrificial love (cf. Mt. 5:39; Rom. 12:17).

Christ enters the world as the tip of the Father's redeeming spear, puncturing the membrane of the world's deceptions and appearing as the Light the 'darkness cannot overcome' (cf. Jn. 1:5).

The body politic rejects Christ like a bad heart transplant. To those who do receive him, however, he gives the power to become *'gods in God'* (cf. Jn. 1:11-12).[30]

Christ has replaced ritual forms of sacrifice with the reconciliation of all things in himself. Cultic expressions of this Mystery exhibit a 'cultic antinomy ', i.e., they use ritual acts to express something that no religious cult can contain.[31]

---

[30] A common theme in the writings of the early church fathers. 'The common goal of the Christian writers of the idealistic orientation was to ascend above the limits of human nature, to become gods through a most intimate union with God ... The idea of deification ... was the central point of the religious life of the Christian East, the point around which revolved all the questions of dogmatics, ethics, and mysticism' V. Kharlamov, *The Idea of Deification in the Early Eastern Church*. See also, Norman Russell, *The Doctrine of Deification in the Greek Patristic Tradition*.

[31] A vision developed by David Fagerberg in his book, *Theologia Prima*.

Christ is a *skandalon* to those who believe that 'might makes right'. Christ is a stumbling block to those who believe 'an eye for an eye and a tooth for a tooth' (cf. Ex. 21:24).

Christ reveals the peace of the world to be institutionalized violence. Politics is simply war by a different name.

Social stability is founded on the sands of mutual distrust. Culture is established on the foundation of murder.[32]

Christ has unmasked our evil deceptions, passing judgment on a world established upon lies and homicide from the beginning (cf. Jn. 8:44; 16:8).

The Light of Christ blinds the clever and the wise, and dissolves, like divine acid, the intellectual hubris of human calculation.

Christ destroys every idol, especially those of political pretense and religious rigor. Christ creates a kingdom of peace in the midst of the world's unending political and religious wars.

---

[32] On murder and the foundation of culture, see René Girard, *The Scapegoat*. See also: https://www.youtube.com/watch?v=6OB4mfR2vCg.

The logic (*Logos*) of God is altogether 'other' than that of the clever and the wise' (cf. 1 Cor. 1:19). God's Wisdom relativizes human wisdom, just as the rising of the sun outshines the light of a candle.

With the revelation of the gospel, it's as if a hypnotic spell has been lifted from the human race. We see, as if for the first time, that blackmail and bribery are the mother's milk of all governance systems, whether secular or sacred.

Disillusionment with every established order is the 'narrow way' into the kingdom of God. Since most of our intellectual constructs are organized illusions, disillusionment is the pathway to peace.

Disenchantment with the ways of the world affords access to the kingdom of God. Embracing disillusionment with the world's wisdom is the *sine quo non* for entering God's Embrace.

Disillusionment is the purification of our hearts' desires. Forsaking the false promises of the world, we discover 'the one thing necessary' (cf. Lk. 10:42).

God is not in competition with anything or anyone, including competition itself.

The Wisdom of God scandalizes all forms of human understanding, but is scandalized by none of them.

The identity of Christ with creation and creation with Christ is as divine and complete as that of Christ with God the Father.

The identity of Christ with the world and the world with Christ is as absolute as Christ's transcendence from the world in the pre-eternal Trinity.

The whole of creation, and humanity in particular, is a creaturely, sophianic extension of the divine-humanity of God's Eternal Word. Creation is naturally 'full of grace', given its origin in, and inseparability from, the eternal divine-humanity of Christ.

Creation is the actualization of the Total Christ (*Totus Christus*). Christ brings creation to completion (cf. Rom. 8:20-21) as the full materialization of his Incarnation (cf. Eph. 1:23; 4:13; Col. 1:28).[33]

Creation exists to give visibility to the Eternal *Logos*. The cosmos is the Mystical Body of Christ, of which Jesus and his church are the heart and soul.

What if St. Paul's extensive use of the phrase 'in Christ' (*en Christo*)[34] is intended *literally*, not metaphorically? What if our 'participation' in Christ's divine humanity assimilates us into God without remainder?[35]

---

[33] **Totus Christus** – Latin phrase meaning the 'whole Christ', and generally used in reference to the relationship between the Son of God and His Body, the Church, which together, bound in spiritual unity, sacramental presence and ordained ministry constitute the Whole Christ. Rooted in the trinitarian perception that even the Divine Persons are complete only in relation with each other, the doctrine of *Totus Christus* maintains that Jesus is complete only in relationship with His Body, the people he has won to Himself. On creation as the completion of the Incarnation, see below, n. 120. See also: Jordan Daniel Wood, *The Whole Mystery of Christ: Creation as Incarnation in Maximus the Confessor*

[34] See the brilliant recapitulation of Pauline realism regarding the phrase *'in Christ'* in James D. G. Dunn, The Theology of Paul the Apostle, 390-410.

[35] Pauline 'mystical realism' is a theme popularized by the agnostic Albert Schweitzer in his groundbreaking book, *The Mysticism of Paul the Apostle* (1931). For an excellent Catholic description and evaluation of the history and current status of the debate regarding Pauline Mysticism, see Romano Penna, *Paul the Apostle: Wisdom and Folly of the Cross.*

Christ is in us *as* us. Corporate humanity is the human face of God, and the glorified cosmos is the transfigured Body of the Total Christ (*Totus Christus*).

Christ is as one with us in his humanity as he is incomparably and incommensurately 'greater' than us as God. Christ is *in us* as God, and we are *in Christ* as *'gods in God'*.[36]

Christ is God's cosmically creative *Logos,* imparting being (existence) and form (essence) to an inestimable array of irreducibly variegated beings (*logoi*).[37]

'God' the 'Father' is the 'Source' (*Archē*) of a trinitarian *Ur-kenosis*.[38] The Father 'dispossesses' himself in the begetting of his Son. The 'Son' 'allows himself' to be begotten,[39] thereby participating in the Father's 'divine relinquishment'.

---

[36] See above, n. 30.

[37] *Logoi* – Greek term with a wide range of meaning, employed in the ancient world to describe the rationality informing the existence of all things and inner principle, essence, or intentionality informing all things, This, in turn, explains the natural participation or fellowship of *logoi* with the *Logos*, who in Scripture is identified as none other than the Son of God Himself, the Father's agent of creation. For a discussion of Maximus the Confessor's description of this relationship, see: Lars Thunberg, *Microcosm and Mediator: The Theological Anthropology of Maximus the Confessor.*

[38] See above, n. 12.

[39] As Adrienne von Speyr says, 'The Son even cooperates in his begetting by *letting* himself be begotten, by holding himself in readiness to be begotten. And within the relationship based on nature, everything is r*epeated on the level of freedom'* (*The*

Jesus *delights* in being begotten of the Father (cf. Mt. 11:25). Jesus' eternal identity is that of 'Eucharist' (*Thanksgiving*). Jesus is 'Eucharist' (in the Trinity) long before making himself a sacrament of the same.

As the 'only-begotten One of God', Christ never 'deemed equality with God something to be grasped at' or possessed (cf. Php. 2:6-11). Instead, he made *creatureliness* the icon of his Sonship, revealing that complete dependence upon the Father, even unto death, is a participation in God's own ecstatically self-surrendering bliss.

The Son's begetting by the Father was *not* an act of deliberation by the Father. The Father was incapable of conceiving of himself without simultaneously begetting his Son.

The Son's generation from the Father is the Father's own self-diffusing nature expressing itself in the act of begetting. It has pleased the Father to eternally beget his Son 'in whom he is always delighted' (cf. Mk. 1:11).

World of Prayer, 75, cited by Hans Urs von Balthasar, *Theo-Drama: Theological Dramatic Theory V*, 87.

The Son's generation by the Father is an act proper to, and expressive of, the Father's own divine *kenosis*. The begetting of the Son comes *naturally* to the Father. Like Father, like Son.

It pleased Christ to aspire to *downward* mobility. Like water, the Son of God gravitates to the lowest place and bids us to do likewise (cf. Lk. 14:9).

To be like water is to be like Christ. Water seeks the lowest place (cf. Lk. 14:9). Water is fully transparent (cf. Jn. 18:12). Water is unassuming (cf. Isa. 53:2). No wonder water (and blood) flowed freely from the pierced heart of Christ on the Cross (cf. Jn. 19:34).

Be like water. Be like Christ. Go with the flow of God's life-giving Spirit. Immerse yourself in the River of Life - it gives growth and produces fruit in every season (cf. Ps. 1:3; Ez. 47:12; Rev. 22:2).

Be like water. Water resists nothing, yet renders buoyant anything empty of itself (cf. Mt. 14:29).

Be like water. Water is stronger than steel. Water is stronger than fire. Water wears down rocks and creates canyons. No wonder Jesus promises that 'fountains of living water' would flow from the hearts of those united to him (cf. Jn. 4:10; 7:38; 15:5).

Our *inability* to desire or accomplish anything good without the grace of God (cf. Php. 2:13) is itself God's gift within us. Our inherent *weakness* as finite creatures is an oblique image of the *Ur-kenosis*[40] at the heart of the Trinity.

Annihilation of self-security is the necessary condition for divine re-creation. Death to self-interest is the prerequisite for deification in God.

---

[40] See above, n. 12. See also: Philip Krill, *Divine Kenosis: Day-by-Day with Hans Urs von Balthasar.*

Sophia

Intuition precedes insight, and insight flows from intuition. Intuition is a fullness of truth whose expression is a prophetic epiphany of God's Holy *Sophia* (Divine Wisdom).

Intuition arises through a sophianic disclosure from an aboriginal Origin (*Ürsprung*). Holy *Sophia* is the mysterious movement of God's Divine Wisdom, inspiring intuition, enabling insight, and leaving no fingerprints from her delicate touch.

Intuitions are divine epiphanies of *Hagia Sophia* (Holy Wisdom). Their power transcends the cognitive abilities of their authors.

Holy Wisdom (*Hagia Sophia*) is Jacob's Ladder (cf. Gen. 28:12) upon which angelic powers move up and down, bringing divine intuition to those chosen by God to know the mind of Christ.

Sophianic intuitions arise suddenly, yet always seem perfectly timed. Those possessed of spiritual intuition know themselves to be humble servants of God's Divine *Sophia*.

God's *Sophia* never stops delivering spiritual intuition to those who await its arrival. More reliable than Old Faithful, Holy Wisdom erupts in the mind of the mystic unbidden, freighted with a prophetic urgency for expression.

Prophets and mystics are cauldrons of intuition. They are possessed of a Holy Wisdom (*Hagia Sophia*) that alights upon them from a Source beyond, yet intimately connected with, themselves.

Divine *Sophia* compels obedience. Spiritual intuitives cannot rest until they give voice to the whispers of the Spirit. Once spoken, their work is finished.

Sophia is the Wisdom of God extended energetically from the heart of the Trinity, making creation capable of receiving God's self-communication.

Sophia is the Source of our eternal élan. *Sophia* is the energy of the Holy Spirit inhabiting us as our ineluctable orientation to the Absolute, which is God.

Sophia is the power of God's Spirit capacitating and disposing us for deified union with God.

Sophia is the WD-40 of the Holy Spirit. *Sophia* makes smooth what is jagged and frees what is stuck.

Sophia is the ever-elusive energy of the Holy Spirit making commerce between the uncreated God and creation possible.

If we are blessed with Holy Wisdom (*Hagia Sophia*), we behold the world as an act of continuous creation by an ineffably loving Source called 'God'. If not, we experience life as a zero-sum game in which we are inexorable losers.

God's *Sophia* inhabits a mystical space between the phenomenal and transcendental realms. With Janus-like vision, those possessed of Divine Wisdom travel up and down Jacob's ladder, making inspired statements without apology or explanation.

Those who experience the immediacy of God's *Sophia* declare, they don't debate. They assert, they don't analyze. They proclaim, they don't explain.

Inspirations arise unbidden in the heart and mind of the maker.[41] Intimations of Divine *Sophia* appear as if from a divine Nowhere, fully formed in depth and breadth, yet awaiting the voice of their recipient to give them adequate expression.

Saints and mystics are possessed of supernatural understanding and saturated with Divine *Sophia*. Not all mystics are saints, nor all saints mystics, but only a person who is neither argues about which is preferable.

Souls saturated with Divine *Sophia* know the Source of their intuitions will never run dry. They speak and write as Wisdom is given to them in real time - never more, never less.

Divine *Sophia* manifests itself in epiphanic fashion. Now you see it, now you don't. So too with the risen Christ: unable to be grasped, he is glimpsed in moments of sophianic awareness.

---

[41] See Dorothy Sayers, *The Mind of the Maker.*

'Learned ignorance' is the precondition for divine illumination. God enlightens the understanding of the lowly but confounds the intelligence of the clever (cf. Mt. 11:25).

Only those willing to be *bewildered* can receive God's *Sophia*. Only those comfortable with paradox, hyperbole, and the union of opposites can perceive the Divine Wisdom that is beyond our concepts of God.

The wisdom of the world is folly (cf. 1 Cor. 3:19) to those touched by Divine *Sophia*.

'Be still and know that I am God' (cf. Ps. 46:10). *Silence* is the ambience of Holy *Sophia*.

The manifestation of *Sophia* is invariably accompanied by gentleness and docility of spirit (cf. Gal. 5:23). Enveloped by God's Holy Wisdom, mystics see the world bathed in the Divine Love that envelop us all (cf. Acts 7:28).

Contemplative prayer dissolves our illusions and divests us of our need and ability to explain anything to anyone. It immerses us in a Divine *Sophia* that is not of this world.

Elevated by God's Divine *Sophia*, we are transported into a world where words are irrelevant and beauty inexpressible.

The words of mystics, anointed as they are with the viscosity of Divine Wisdom, are smooth and effortless. For mystics, it is only a matter of allowing Holy *Sophia* to utter her words of wisdom through them.

As the mystic's vision expands to include the entire horizon of human history, it also narrows to an indefinable point of uncreated light from whence flows Divine *Sophia*. Mystics are humbled by a sense of their own nothingness, while at the same time they are filled with the bliss of Divine *Sophia*.

Prophets and mystics are sentinels of the Unspeakable. They stand vigilant in the silence of the spirit, awaiting the arrival of Holy *Sophia*. They are the selfless servants of God's sophianic epiphanies.

Mystics are given the Holy Wisdom (*Hagia Sophia*) to elusively express what registers opaquely in their souls. They realize that no expression, however eloquent, oblique or paradoxical, can adequately manifest what they intuit.

The Desire of our desires is the Spirit of God within us. We are possessed of the Life and Love of God, yet ignorant of this fact until our minds are illumined by Divine *Sophia*.

Wisdom arises in the heart of the saint like a divine geyser whose eruptions are as arresting as they are regular. Never taken for granted, yet always anticipated and appreciated, the wisdom of the saints is a participation in God's own elusively reliable Divine *Sophia*.

Our awareness of God's Presence is a manifestation of God's Holy *Sophia*. If we are wise to the things of the Spirit, it is because God's Wisdom has made us so.

God and creation are co-inherent without conflation. The world is in God and God is in the world, yet the world is not God and God is not the world. Understanding this is a work of God's Holy *Sophia* (Wisdom).

Our desire to know God is God's own Spirit sophianically active within us. Our deification is undertaken and perfected by God's Divine *Sophia*.

By virtue of its very existence, creation shimmers with Divine *Sophia*. Divine *Sophia* reveals the world as a sacrament of God's self-communication.

Our *entelechy*[42] as creatures is a participation in the Wisdom of God. Our capacity for becoming 'partakers of the divine nature' (cf. 2 Pt. 1:4) is a participation in God's Holy *Sophia*.

Mystics are filled with gratitude for having discovered 'the one thing necessary' (cf. Lk. 10:42). Filled with Divine Wisdom (Holy *Sophia*), they experience themselves as 'gods in God'.[43]

Those possessed of Divine *Sophia* know that God, as the Source of all that exists, is devoid of anything but Light and Love. For the mystic, matter is congealed goodness, creation is solidified light, and humanity is miniaturized Divine Love.

Like a high-end supermarket employing a gentle hydration system to keep its produce fresh, the soul of the mystic is irrigated from within with the soft spray of God's *Sophia*. The fruit produced by such a soul contains more spiritual nutrients and enriching goodness than any fare found in the religious marketplace.

---

[42] **Entelechy** is a Greek term meaning the vital principle that guides the development and functioning of an organism or other system or organization.
[43] See above, n. 30.

Divine *Sophia* is a Spirit of simplification. Those possessed of God's Wisdom let go of anything and anyone that impairs their unconditional service to the intuitions that possess them.

Mystics sustain a sense of the 'gratuity of being'. They abide in a world of Divine Wisdom (*Sophia*) where possessiveness finds no purchase.

Mystics know that zero-sum thinking is a lie. Illumined by Divine *Sophia*, they exhibit an unquenchable joy and fearless trust that 'all will be well, and all manner of things will be well'.[44]

Every prophet, every mystic works without a net. They walk a tightrope in the heavens that those watching from below can only gasp at.

Mystics know it's better to light one candle than to curse the darkness. Divine Wisdom is a light in the heart of the mystic which the darkness cannot overcome (cf. Jn. 1:5).

---

[44] Julian of Norwich, *Revelations of Divine Love.*

Mystics enjoy a kind of holy amnesia. Enlightened by holy *Sophia*, they view every failure as an opportunity. They abide in the light of an unspeakably blissful future (*Plērōma*)[45] that leaves the past in the rear view mirror.

Mystics move about with an intuitive self-possession, bringing light and joy wherever they go. Interiorly united to their Source, they become, effortlessly, instruments of Divine *Sophia*.

Mystics have an inner ear attuned to Divine *Sophia*. They hear dog-whistles of the Spirit inaccessible to normal perception.

Like persons with OCD, those possessed of Divine *Sophia* can tell when any situation is off-kilter. They cringe with compassion for those who 'cannot see what they see and who cannot hear what they hear' (cf. Ps. 115:5).

Mystics abide peacefully in the Cloud of Unknowing.[46] They embrace the 'passive night of the spirit',[47] gladly submitting themselves to the purifying fire of God's unrelenting love.

---

[45] *Plērōma* – Greek word translated 'fullness', or 'totality'. In Scripture (cf. Jn. 1:12-14; Eph. 1:22-23; Col. 1:19; 2:9-10), it refers to the fullness of God in Christ and the recapitulation and redemption of all things in Christ.

[46] See above, n. 14.

[47] See St. John of the Cross, *Dark Night of the Soul*.

Infused with Divine *Sophia*, we can trust God will glorify us to the extent, and in the same measure, that our deification will glorify God.

Those possessed of *Sophia* live in the epicenter of the Now. Theirs is a moment-to-moment reliance on a Power greater than themselves.

Those infused with Divine *Sophia* have learned to trust the 'still, small voice' within (cf. 1 Kg. 19:12). They exhibit the innocence of children and the wisdom of the sage (cf. Mt. 10:16; 18:3).

Mystics speak in *pericopes*[48] - short, self-contained utterances aimed at the heart. Once their spiritual arrows are shot, mystics withdraw from the action, receding into the luminous darkness from whence their inspiration derives.

Mystics are allergic to spiritual cliches. They abhor spiritual systems. Immersed in God's *Sophia*, they eschew every off-the-shelf spiritual remedy promoted by flash-in-the-pan preachers.

---

[48] *Pericope* is a set of verses that forms one coherent unit or thought, suitable for public reading from a text, now usually of sacred scripture. .

Those filled with God's *Sophia* gravitate to the lowest place (cf. Lk. 14:9). They prefer *hiddenness* to the flashing lights of social media.

St. Francis prayed to become an instrument of God's peace. Mystics pray to be ever-clearer channels of God's Divine *Sophia*.

It is one thing to love God in all things, quite another to love all things *in God*.[49] The former is the way of the saint, the latter the mystical way of Divine *Sophia*.

Mystics operate in a sophianic space connecting this world to the kingdom of God. They make no definitive judgments about human states of affairs, but see all things as backlit by God's illuminative Wisdom.

Mystics experience the world as a sacrament of divine Presence. God's *Sophia* reveals that nature itself has no real existence apart from God, and that only as 'grace' can what is 'natural' possess any actuality at all.

---

[49] As St. John of the Cross says, The deified soul 'knows [created] things better in God's being that in themselves ... The soul knows creatures through God and not God through creatures' (*Living Flame of Love*, Stanza IV. 5, emphasis added).

Divine *Sophia* alights upon a person like the Holy Spirit enveloped the Virgin Mary (cf. Lk. 1:35). Wisdom comes to us as utterly unconditioned, imbued with unfathomable goodness.

Mystics know that, ontologically speaking, God is all that is. Divine *Sophia* shows us that whatever is 'not God' exists as an extension and expression of God's own divine Life.

A true prophet needs to be a mystic, and a genuine mystic - i.e., one possessed of *Sophia* - has no choice other than to prophesy.

There is an inner unction in the heart of the mystic which continually releases an anointing of Divine Mercy. *Sophia* is a release of spiritual viscosity, enabling the mystic to see the world through soft eyes.

Gentleness is a leading characteristic of Divine *Sophia*. Giving others the benefit of the doubt comes naturally to those infused with God's Wisdom.

Quibbling about political correctness is anathema to the mystic's vision. True Wisdom (*Sophia*) rises above the world of dialectical discourse.

Sophia circumvents the divisions and dichotomies of a rivalrous humanity. It rests beautifully in an eschatological vision of the reconciliation of all things in the Total Christ (*Totus Christus*).[50]

Mystics understand that God's *Sophia* governs the genesis, generation and gestation of their revelations. Mystics know that when they give expression to their experience, it is 'the Father speaking through them' (cf. Mt. 10:20).

Those who, through Divine *Sophia*, know God as a Mystery of Divine *Kenosis*,[51] also know how to stay in their own lane. Their expectations of themselves are minimal, while their confidence in their personal mission is unlimited (cf. Php. 4:13).

Every word and action that pours forth from the heart of a mystic is rich with Divine *Sophia* and pregnant with Divine Love. How they do anything is how they do everything.

---

[50] See above, n. 33.

[51] See above, n. 40.

Mystics live a sacramental life. Their ordinary actions bespeak a secret, sacred depth, touching the lives of those who know them. They exhibit a *Sophia* the world does not understand (cf. Sir. 20:30; 1 Cor. 2:7).

Mystics imitate no one. They delight in their singularity and consider all comparisons odious. They know their lives are 'hidden with Christ in God' (cf. Col. 3:3).

Mystics traverse the world with the unobtrusiveness of a Zen master walking on rice paper. Those possessed of Divine *Sophia* treat the ills of the world with the delicacy of a surgeon's touch.

Saints listen to the Wisdom of God with the ear of a mother attuned to the breathing of her sleeping child. *Sophia* is the silent whispering of the Holy Spirit.

Mystics hear the silent music of Divine *Sophia*. They are attuned to Spirit-filled whispers more alluring and imperceptible than the siren songs of the fallen world.

Mystics weep over the ways of the world, but their tears turn to joy (cf. Ps. 126:5; Jn. 16:20) when they glimpse the least indication of love. The world is too much for them, and they are too much for the world.

Divine *Sophia* immunizes us from following the crowd.[52] It teaches us to go with the Flow - the flow of 'the River of Life' - 'for the healing of the nations' (cf. Rev. 22:2).

Demonization is the world's default dynamic for ensuring peace. Those enlightened with Divine *Sophia* refuse to participate.

Illumined with Divine *Sophia*, we abide with the God 'in whom there is no darkness' (cf. 1 Jn. 1:5). Filled with the Wisdom of God, we enjoy a peace, joy, and hope the world cannot give (cf. 1 Jn. 1:5).

Joy is the infallible sign of those illumined with Divine *Sophia*. Such persons exhibit self-love without self-interest, and they can be self-critical without being self-condemning.

---

[52] For Jesus' aversion to 'the crowd' as the occasion of sin, see Robert Hamerton-Kelly's book, *The Gospel and the Sacred: Poetics of Violence in Mark*.

Imbued with Divine *Sophia*, saints know that everyone lives in glass houses, that nobody should throw stones. They know that 'apart from God we can do nothing' (cf. Jn. 15:5) but that, in Christ, 'all things are possible' (cf. Php. 4:13; Mt. 19:26).

If we acquire sophianic vision, everything is eternally fresh, eternally perfect. *Sophia* shows us that 'behold, God makes all things new!' (cf. Rev. 21:5).

Infused with Divine *Sophia*, it's as if we are continually witnessing the Big Bang, saying with God, 'It is good, very good!' (cf. Gen. 1:31).

God's *Sophia* reveals to the childlike what is hidden from the clever and the wise (cf. Mt. 11:25).

PART TWO

HUMANITAS

Hamartia

No rational creature can intentionally do evil.[53] This alone should give us pause when passing judgment on others.

The Evil one is a 'liar and murderer from the beginning' (cf. Jn. 8:44). Devils may be demented and destructive, but their destiny is to be united with God.

Why regard the failures of others as anything other than deceived aspirations to attain the Good, the Fullness of which is found in God?

---

[53] 'Evil cannot be intended by anyone for its own sake; but it can be intended for the sake of avoiding another evil, or obtaining another good…and in this case anyone would choose to obtain a good intended for its own sake, without suffering loss of the other good; even as a lustful man would wish to enjoy pleasure without offending God…' (St. Thomas Aquinas, *Summa Theologica*, II-I.7.8.1.) For Aquinas, any inclination towards evil is always 'due to corruption or disorder' in one of the basic 'principles' of human constitution: ignorance in reason, unbridled desire for gratification, or the defect in the will of loving a lesser good over a greater one, but always intending something good.

Social justice warriors tend to curse the darkness more often than they light a candle. In this way the Deceiver piggybacks upon prophets of injustice, turning victims into persecutors and deceiving everyone in their mutual self-righteousness.

Christ enjoins resistance to evil but not retaliation. He urges the acceptance of suffering but not indifference (cf. Mt. 5:39; Rom. 12:21). It's difficult to resist evil without using the instruments of evil, or to suffer injustice without seeking revenge.

It's no easy matter to acquire 'the innocence of a dove and the cunning of the serpent' (cf. Mt. 10:16). It takes a lifetime of letting-go to be able to be 'in the world but not of it' (cf. Jn. 15:19).

The Uncreated Light of God puts to shame all attempts to see others in a negative light. 'God is Light in whom there is no darkness' (cf. 1 Jn. 1:5).

Light and darkness are not co-equal Powers. Light exists, darkness does not. Why consider the *absence* of light as anything substantial?

Darkness is without substance. Evil is never anything other than a *deprivation* of the good.

Nothing that is good can be destroyed, nothing that is evil can endure. Therein lies the peace of God.[54]

Sin is blindness to our teleological orientation to God. Sin is ignorance of self-transcendence, the perfection of which is eternal beatitude.

Sin is the illusion of self-sufficiency, of self-enclosed systems, of a self-explanatory existence. Sin is the failure to see, to delight in, and to be be humbled by our intrinsic neediness, our inherent dependence.

Our spiritual desire is insatiable. Sin is the inability to discern our tacit desire for God as the Absolute Good in our every thought, word and action.

Sin is essentially self-deception, i.e., a failure to see that we are forever seeking a satisfaction in created goods that only the Absolute Good ('God') can give.

---

[54] A paraphrase of the opening lines of *A Course in Miracles*: 'Nothing real can be threatened, and nothing unreal exists. Therein lies the peace of God'.

In no way is evil the ontological opposite of divine Goodness. Pitting Satan against God as worthy adversaries is Manichean nonsense.[55]

Sin is the ignorance, arrogance, insolence, and uncomprehending sense of entitlement of those who lack self-awareness. God only knows what their awakening will take.

To 'hate sin' is to immerse ourselves more fully in it, just as to 'pursue holiness' is to run a fool's errand. Neither vice nor virtue is of much interest to God.

Those who abide in God '*cannot* sin' (cf. 1 Jn. 3:9), nor do they regard ethical achievement as anything other than 'so much rubbish' (cf. Gal. 3:10; Php. 3:8).

Our sin is God's opportunity. Where 'sin increases', God's gracious restorative goodness 'abounds even more' (cf. Rom. 5:20).

---

[55] *Manichaeism* teaches an elaborate dualistic cosmology describing the struggle between a good, spiritual world of light, and an evil, material world of darkness. It imputes to darkness a power substantially equal and opposite to that of divine Light. It is a perversion of Christian faith as popular implicitly in practice today as it was in the patristic age of the church.

The mystical Body of Christ (*Corpus Mysticum*) suffers the internecine violence of its members. Criticism and condemnation are the invectives championed by 'blind guides' (cf. Mt. 15:14), impervious to their own resentments and penchant for retaliation.

Desire is of God, but *desire for the goods of another* is of the evil one. Only Jesus and Mary were completely free of covetousness and its resultant sin of envy.

God is beyond opposites, yet the polarities and dualities in creation (yin and yang, equal and opposites) reflect God's trinitarian beatitude.

Evil is an inverse image of divine benevolence. For those with 'eyes to see' (cf. Lk. 10:32), chaos and calamity, no less than unity and order, point us towards God.

If we can remain relaxed and centered in God, giving what threatens us enough space to punch itself out, we will see 'Satan fall like lightening' (cf. Lk. 10:18).

Because no one can intentionally do evil without intending good,[56] every sin is committed in ignorance. Is this not why Jesus said, 'Father, forgive them, they *know not* what they are doing' (cf. Lk. 23:34)?

The road to hell is paved with good intentions. Self-deception is at the heart of every sin.

Evil is nothing but human nature throwing a hissy-fit. Like a good mother, God holds an out-of-control humanity in his Divine Embrace until it cries itself to sleep.

The more evil escalates, the more saints de-escalate. Christ invites us to 'overcome evil with good' (cf. Rom. 12:21), knowing that 'a kind answer turns away wrath' (cf. Prov. 15:1).

Evil cannot be destroyed, it can only be dissolved. Christ came, not to demolish, but to disarm, the 'principalities and powers' of evil (cf. Eph. 3:10).

---

[56] See above, n. 53.

Evil possesses the reality of a magician's trick - the masking of the truth with a studied deception. When we fall for the Evil One's illusions, the trick is on us.

Evil is a demonic sleight of hand with no more substance than that of a Vegas magician. Still, it scares the hell out of people.

Sin is essentially unconsciousness. Failing self-awareness, we live a flat-earth reality, incapable of knowing the difference between reacting and responding.

Sin is our *default*, not our 'natural', condition. Our *natural* condition is as the 'image and likeness of God' (cf. Gen. 1:26), filled with the love and light of our Creator.[57]

Sinners possess negligible situational awareness. Saints, by contrast, are self-aware and self-possessed.

---

[57] 'In the terms of the great Maximus the Confessor (c. 580–662), the 'natural will' within us, which is the rational ground of our whole power of volition, must tend only toward God as its true end, for God is goodness as such, whereas our 'gnomic' or 'deliberative' will can stray from him, but only to the degree that it has been blinded to the truth of who he is and what we are, and as a result has come to seek a false end as its true end.' (David Bentley Hart, *That All Shall Be Saved: Heaven, Hell, and Universal Salvation*, 36.)

Our every sin is God's opportunity. God has 'consigned all to disobedience (sin) so he may show mercy to all' (cf. Rom. 11:32).

Better to light a single candle than to curse the darkness. Christ is God's candle, enflamed by the Holy Spirit, offering hope to a world wrapped in darkness.

The temptation to explore the depths of the world's darkness is of a piece with the darkness itself. Only a deified person dares describe the darkness without being co-opted by it.

Everyone is a tacit tyrant who does not approach life as a servant. Unsolicited advice is covert criticism.

Do-gooders are often deceived by their own good intentions. In this, they mirror the self-righteousness of those whose injustices they seek to correct.

Victimization is often weaponized to victimize others. As the ancient maxim puts it: 'No worse master than a former slave'.

The dynamics of resentment and retaliation destroy those who fall prey to their central lie, i.e., that two wrongs make a right.

'Divide and conquer' - this is every tyrant's favorite tool. Deceive, demonize, divide and destroy - this is the logic of those who have not discovered the *Logos* (logic) of God.

Questions are God's gentle way of awakening the world from its nightmare of retaliative violence. Head-on assault with evil never works, since it is playing the world's game of tit-for-tat, eye-for-an-eye.

The catharsis violence provides is anathema in the kingdom of God. The fundamental lie of violence is unmasked when violence is allowed to show its ugly face at the expense of the innocent (cf. Mk. 15:39).

Water breaks down concrete by gently entering, then expanding, cracks in the facade. God works in a similar way, gently, gradually transforming our hardened hearts.

'You shall know the truth and the truth will set you free' (cf. Jn. 8:32). Truth is a sophianic extension of the Wisdom of God, 'condemning the world of its sin' and setting the world free from its 'slavery to sin' (cf. Jn. 8:34; Rom. 6:18; Heb. 2:15).

Truth is translated as 'un-concealed-ness', 'disclosure', 'revealing', or 'un-closed-ness.'[58] Truth unmasks our illusions, disarms us of our sins, and debunks our explanations.

Truth *shows* what cannot be said. Truth is *self-evidently* beautiful, *compelling* our consent. Truth always leaves us speechless.

Truth unveils our ignorance. Truth banishes our darkness. Truth removes our confusion so that the primordial goodness of being can show itself.

The dynamic of sin can be summed up by the 4R's, the 4C's and the 4F's: Rivalry, resentment, rage, retribution; Comparison, criticism, complaint, condemnation; Fight, force, fix, figure out.

---

[58] 'Truth' is *Aletheia* (ἀλήθείἀ) in Greek.

The cycle of reciprocal violence is as unbreakable as it is unconscious. Only being ashamed by how we behave saves us from our sins.

Christ shames us on the Cross by offering himself as the innocent victim of human violence. The Cross unmasks our mendacity and manifests God's Divine Mercy.

The Cross of Christ is God's mirror, showing the murderous face of humanity, and revealing the face of God as forgiveness (cf. Lk. 24:34).

Invitation is at the heart of human nature. *Welcoming* is what allows us to bloom. Sin has replaced invitation with intimidation; sin has twisted welcoming into wariness.

Recapturing the innocence of a child is the work of a lifetime. Acquiring a second naïveté,[59] permeated with uncynical wisdom, is the achievement of the saint.

---

[59] 'Beyond rational and critical thinking, we need to be called again. This can lead to the discovery of a 'second naïveté', which is a return to the joy of our first naïveté, but now totally new, inclusive, and mature thinking'. (Paul Ricœur, 1913–2005).

Sin is always a function of ignorance, which itself is a result of deception. Culpability, as we account it, is found nowhere in God's calculus of our moral or ontological worth.

What is the 'sin against the Holy Spirit' (cf. Lk. 10:10), if not the belief that any sin is unforgivable?

Where do we get the penitentiary notion of eternal torment as God's ultimate trump card, if not from the Evil One himself?

What criminological catechesis is it that teaches that the all-redeeming Mystery of Christ is rendered impotent because of an insuperable boundary fixed by human sin?

It is theological nonsense to insist that our sins prevent Christ from emptying Hades of its poor, unfortunate inhabitants. How, otherwise, could the apostle proclaim, 'O hell, where is your victory?' (cf. 1 Cor. 15:55; Hos. 13:14)?

When the seriousness of sin is used to frighten us with the threat of conscious, eternal torment, it is a fruitless activity unworthy of human beings. We are created, called and destined for ultimate, ecstatic union with God.

It is our very *vulnerability* to sin that endears us to God. What Divine Physician would refuse to save the lives of the most seriously ill?

Why did Jesus say, 'Those who are well have no need of a physician, but those who are sick' (Lk. 5:31), if not because, in all situations, he prefers mercy to sacrifice (cf. Hos. 6:6; Mt. 9:13; 12:7)?

Could it be that God created a human race *liable* to the sickness of sin so his Son could manifest his glory by healing our wounds (cf. Ps. 147:3)? Could it be that God created a world in need of mercy so that his Son, the Divine Mercy, would not exist in vain?[60]

Every sin must be expiated, the *purpose* of which is our salvation (cf. 1 Cor. 3:15). The fires of hell are real, the refining *aim* of which is our redemption.

Those who argue for everlasting punishment for sins are seeking vengeance, not justice. Divine justice is always restorative, never retributive. God wounds only to heal (cf. Job 5:18).

---

[60] See above, n. 21.

Infernalists[61] lack an anagogical vision in which 'every knee shall bow to God, and every tongue shall give praise to God' (Rom.14:11), 'whether in heaven, on earth, or under the earth' (cf. Php. 2:11).

Infernalists lack a sense of 'final causality'.[62] The fail to appreciate that God created the world with the *Totus Christus* (Total Christ) in mind, i.e., a *Plērōma* of universal recreation in which God himself is 'all in all' (cf. 1 Cor. 15:28-29).

It offends both reason and faith to accept the idea of infinite punishment and eternal torment for *any amount* of finite and limited sins. This pedagogy of theological terror is perhaps the greatest of sins.

It's a great relief to realize that politics is nothing more than organized crime.

---

[61] A term coined by David Bentley Hart: 'The great majority of defenders of the idea of a real hell of eternal torment (for brevity's sake, we can call them 'infernalists' hereafter) never really get around to addressing properly the question of whether we can make moral sense of God's acts in the great cosmic drama of creation, redemption, and damnation (*That All Shall Be Saved: Heaven, Hell, and Universal Salvation*, 12-13).

[62] Following Aristotle, a four-fold notion of causality has been used by St. Thomas Aquinas and others to shed light on the anagogical purposes of God: material causes, efficient causes, formal causes, and final causes. A *final* cause is the purpose (*telos*) for which something is crated. Infernalists beg the question: 'Why would God create persons in his own image and likeness for the purpose of their final damnation or annihilation?'.

God allows us to exhaust ourselves with sin to awaken within us a passion for the One who alone is Good (cf. Mk. 10:18). Where sin abounds, grace abounds even more (cf. Rom. 5:20).

Christ, like God, has no deliberative (*gnomic*) will, and thus is incapable of sin.[63] Sin is inevitable for us who require deliberation and, therefore, make countless poor, sinful choices.

Conformity to Christ is the dissolution of the deliberative (*gnomic*) will and acquisition of 'the mind of Christ' (cf. Php. 2:5; Gal. 2:20). For those so conformed, sin is impossible (cf. 1 Jn. 3:9).

Freedom and necessity are identical in God. So too for those who 'abide in God' (cf. 1 Jn. 4:16). Because they abide in 'perfect love', they neither fear nor sin (cf. 1 Jn. 4:18; 3:9).

---

[63] The concept of the *gnomic*, or deliberative, will is a central point in the Christology of St. Maximus the Confessor (580-662). According to Maximus, if human nature required the real capacity freely to reject God, then Christ could not have been fully human. Christ, however, *is* fully human and fully free. He possesses no *gnomic* (deliberative) will because his will was perfectly free from the need to deliberate or decide between right or wrong, truth or error, good or evil. Christ was - as we should all wish to become - incapable of any deviation from the Good. Christ had a perfect knowledge of the Good and was thus perfectly rational. As a fully human being, Christ could not sin; hence, he alone among men was fully free. See Lars Thunberg, *Microcosm and Mediator: The Theological Anthropology of Maximus the Confessor.*

Freedom is not the spasmodic exercise of 'free choice', otherwise there would be no difference between the saint and the serial killer. Sin is the use of our agency untethered to the truth of God.

Demonic freedom is unfettered, unlimited, arbitrary choice. Divine freedom is tethered to the truth.

Demonic freedom is a libertarian, voluntaristic exercise of pure will, impervious to anything other than self-satisfaction. Divine freedom is delightfully obedient - inspired by a vision of the good, true and beautiful that compels love and surrender.

Sin is a *forfeiture* of our freedom - not as the misuse of our agency, but as ignorance of 'the truth' that 'sets us free from our slavery to sin' (cf. Jn. 8:32-34).

Saints have discovered true freedom - i.e., not the unfettered ability to choose, but the *inability* to choose anything not given them by God's Divine *Sophia*.

Unbridled libertarian freedom, defined as the ability to do what one wills, as one wills and when one wills, is a demonic illusion. Human agency, empty of anything but self-assertion, is satanic.[64]

Any action (say, choosing to have an abortion) or any belief (say, choosing to believe in hell as a place of everlasting, conscious torment) based on a voluntaristic notion of freedom as an unfettered capacity to choose, is the very definition of sin.

Luciferian freedom is that of pure will, i.e., doing what one wants just because one can. Who but deluded narcissists would reject God's offer of eternal life simply to demonstrate their power?

Resistance to God's grace is not sin but insanity.

True freedom is both a gift and a task, a capacity and an achievement. Freedom itself needs to be set free by knowing and doing the truth (cf. Gal. 5:1; Jn. 8:32-36).

---

[64] See: The Open Ark, 2024. '*Apokatastasis: Part II - on Theophanism*'. May 1, 2024. https://theopenark.substack.com/p/apokatastasis-part-ii.

All the sin in the world can neither mortally wound, nor even touch, the innermost image and likeness of God within us.

Sin, and the hellish misery it brings, is nothing more than ignorance of our essential identity in, and desire for, God.

Hardness of heart - sin - is no insuperable obstacle to God's efficient grace.[65] The Living Water can penetrate, and dissolve, the most resistant will.

Who can explain purity of heart? Only God sees our deepest intentions. Beneath all our desires is an unrestricted desire for God.

The person God has made each of us to be - conceived in God before the foundation of the world (cf. Eph. 1:4) - remains forever untouched and untouchable by sin.

Our conscience can never be killed because our intrinsic connection with God can never be broken.

---

[65] See: Love Unrelenting. 2021. *'Is Hard-Heartedness of Heart a Good Argument for an Everlasting Hell?'* - Eric Reitan. Www.youtube.com. September 30, 2021. https://www.youtube.com/watch?v=v2SFrnBuO5Q&t=634s.

Conscience accuses us only to save us from our sins. Conscience is the *Sophia* of God, gently reawakening us to our essential, eternal identity in God.

Salvation is the purpose of all suffering. Otherwise, God would not allow it.

Sin obscures *our* awareness of our virginal beauty in God's eyes, but has no power to efface the unique, personal identity God has given each of us.

The greatest sin is to believe sin itself could ever separate us from the redemptive love of Christ (cf. Rom. 8:39). Either God 'has consigned all to disobedience so he can show mercy to all' (cf. Rom. 11:32) or he has not.

Those who make the power of sin equal to that of God question either God's omnipotence or God's goodness. Are not these the ones 'who have the greater sin' (cf. Jn. 19:11)?

Can sin and evil be considered ontological equals and opposites of the goodness and love of God? If so, the jury is still out on who is more powerful, God or the devil.

Sin is a departure from the truth of our true being, a departure from the truth of God. How can any *'departure'* be as *real* as the 'Way' and the 'Life' (cf. Jn. 15:15) that makes such a 'departure' possible?

Sin is always a perversion of something good. Evil is always parasitic upon that which it seeks, in vain, to destroy. In themselves, neither sin nor evil has any real substance.

Sin is inherently self-subversive. All sentient creatures, including the demons, eventually get sick and tired of being sick and tired.

In the Uncreated Light of God's truth, we cannot but be horrified by our sins. Yet, our very capacity to be horrified presumes a deeper, *redemptive purpose* of this hellish revelation, i.e., our ultimate union with God.

Seeing the discrepancy between who we are in God's pre-eternal conception of us (cf. Ps. 139:13; Jer. 1:5) and what we have become through our sins is a hellish experience. It is made possible by the same God who, through this crucible of divine judgment, 'makes all things new' (cf. Rev. 21:5).

The Word of God is a 'two-edged sword, separating joint from marrow' (cf. Heb. 4:12). It excises the cancer of sin from our souls, causing us insuperable pain, while simultaneously saving our souls from death (cf. Ps. 33:19; 68:20).

Might not the greatest sin be to presume that the misuse of human agency could defeat Christ's anagogical assumption of humanity into the glorious *Plērōma*[66] of God (cf. Jn. 12:32; Rom. 5:18; 8:32)?

Strictly speaking, it is not 'sins' that are forgiven, but sinners. This inviolable distinction is at once our indictment and exoneration in the eyes of God.

If how we do anything is how we do everything, then everything we do is a mixture of weeds and wheat, sin and goodness (cf. Mt. 13:29-30). Only a *grim* reaper, not the infinitely *gracious* God, would burn the weeds without saving the wheat.

Scripture is a narrative, either of God's salvation of the world in Christ (cf. Jn. 4:42; 6:51), or the triumph of sin over the redemptive desire of God (cf. 2 Tim. 1:4). 'Shall the axe vaunt itself over him who hews with it, or the saw magnify itself against him who wields it?' (Isa. 10:15).

---

[66] See above, n. 45.

Saints know that no sin can ever be truly mortal. Sin deserves as little attention as the loving father gave to the prepared confession of his prodigal son (cf. Lk. 15:18-24).

In our sin, we imagine God consigning sinners to everlasting torment. In this we are deceived. God's so-called 'punishment of sins' is the purification of our hearts for the salvation of our souls (cf. 1 Cor. 3:15).

How can the exposure of our sins to the consuming fire of God's Love (cf. Heb. 12:29) result in anything less than their complete conflagration?

How can the incineration of our impurities in God's Presence (cf. Rev. 21:27) be anything less than the salvation of our lives which are 'hidden with Christ in God' (cf. Col. 3:3)?

'God is the light in whom there is no darkness' (cf. 1 Jn. 1:5). God exposes evil as nothing but an absence of light.

Justice and mercy are identical in God. The so-called 'punishment' of God is the purifying fire of God's Divine Mercy.

The 'wrath' of God is the 'holy hell' permitted by God to deliver us from the suffering that follows naturally from our sins. Once the dross is burned away, we shine with the glory given us before the foundation of the world.

Without being indifferent to the self-destructive ways of the human race, God is beyond being offended by the human persons he has created as fallible and capable of evil. The anger of Christ (cf. Mk. 3:5) is driven by a human grief (cf. Lk. 19:41) and rooted in divine, redemptive compassion (cf. Isa. 44:21; 49:15).

God is not schizophrenic. He doesn't choose us 'before the foundation of the world to be holy and blameless in his sight' (cf. Eph. 1:4), then discard us at the end of time because we have not lived up to our calling.

Theosis

'God became man so man could become God'.[67] *Theosis* - deification - is the purpose of both the Incarnation and creation.

Christ's *kenosis* (self-donation) is our *theosis* (divinization).

Our purpose and destiny as God's 'image and likeness' (cf. Gen. 1:26) is to become 'partakers of God's divine nature' (cf. 2 Pt. 1:4). Only a humanity that is *always already divine* can become God.[68]

We are naturally hard-wired to seek the Good, the Source and Sum of which is Absolute Goodness, i.e., God. Our 'natural', orientation towards God *is* the Presence of God already in possession of us.

---

[67] St. Athanasius, *On the Incarnation*, 54.
[68] One of the main themes of David Bentley Hart's book, *You Are Gods: On Nature and Supernature*.

Both our desire for, and power to achieve, the good are altogether God's doing (cf. Php. 2:13). It is folly, not humility, to imagine that our misuse of freedom can defeat God's desire that 'all persons be saved and come to a knowledge of the truth' (cf. 1 Tim. 2:4).

Holy desire is holiness itself. Our desire for God *is* God's self-communication through the medium of desire.

The act of *deference* is at the heart of the Trinity. Creating and holding the space for others to be themselves is the earmark of God's divinity and our *theosis*.

The spiritual practice of *adab* (courtesy) is both a means and by-product of *theosis*. Deification issues necessarily in gentleness of spirit (cf. Gal. 5:23).

Deified persons reveal the Presence of God just by walking around. They experience themselves as unrestricted 'fields of self-presence' whose simplest gestures encourage the flourishing of others.

Self-forgetfulness is a by-product of being inwardly oriented to the Mystery of God. *Theosis* redounds to those who bring their horizontal activities - thoughts, actions, annoyances, difficulties, etc. - into alignment with their intuitive apprehension of God.

Focus on God as the Source of existence is the ultimate catalyst for self-forgetfulness, just as self-forgetfulness (*kenosis*) is at the heart of God's own Divine Life (cf. Php. 2:6-11).[69]

God is intuitively apprehended by every person everywhere at all times. *Theosis* is largely a matter of making this divine intuition explicit without reification.

Saints see with the eyes of God. With deified vision,[70] they perceive the inherent perfection in everything God has created.

Everything we have by way of holiness is a by-product of God's self-serving beneficence. It is because God alone is good (cf. Mk. 10:18) that we are good by our *participation in* God.

---

[69] On the subject of God's *Ur-kenosis* (originate self-dispossession), see above, n. 12.

[70] *See: Philip Krill, Deified Vision: Towards an Anagogical Catholicism.*

Because it has pleased God to never be without us (cf. Eph. 1:4; Jn. 14:3), nothing can separate us from the divinizing love of God (cf. Rom. 8:39). God desires our deification more than we ever can.

A saint is immune from argumentation, yet acutely aware of evil and dysfunction. *Theosis* makes one 'as wise as a serpent and innocent as a dove' (cf. Mt. 10:16).

The unique, bewildering singularity of the saint is an icon of the ineffable God who eludes description and avoids all human discord.

Greed is anathema to divinized persons. For them, less is always more. Theirs is a fullness of joy at every moment.

As connoisseurs of the present moment, deified persons savor life. A single taste of what the world has to give is all they need or desire.

Saints experience the pleasures of life as the *hors d'oeuvres* of a heavenly banquet. 'Fasting' from the insipid fare of this world, deified persons save themselves for the Wedding Feast of the Lamb (cf. Rev. 19:9).

With joy, surprise and amazement, saints recognize the giftedness of all that arises, giving them a freedom that is the opposite of spasmodic impulse.

Deified persons have little or no need for deliberation. They know intuitively how to handle situations that previously baffled them.[71]

Theosis is co-natural alignment with the truth (cf. Jn. 16:13). Those divinized by God's Spirit apprehend the truth that sets them free - free from hesitation, indecision and deception (cf. 2 Cor. 1:19).

Saints have no interest in keeping all their options open. They have found 'the road less traveled' and they have taken it without looking back.

Saints have no opinions. They proclaim, they don't explain. They leave the act of interpretation to those who still confuse argumentation with apprehension.

---

[71] A paraphrase of one of the Promises of *Alcoholics Anonymous*.

If saints worry at all, it's about doing anything unaligned with their awareness of God's Presence. Their anxiety is of a piece with Jesus' agony in the garden: they sweat blood at the prospect that, in a moment of weakness, they might betray the Divine Love that possesses them.

In the depths of one's spirit, the saint hears, 'Be!'. The internal axis of a saint's existence is his or her abiding, blissful awareness that 'I am' because 'God is'.

Saints apprehend God as Absolute Goodness - the Source and Center of their being. In their hearts, they know that, because 'God is good', it is infinitely good that they exist.

A saint's intuition of the unconditioned graciousness of being is the taproot of their deification. They realize that 'I am' because 'God is'.

Saints enjoy a kind of 'second sight'. They intuit the glorious recapitulation of all things in Christ (cf. 1 Cor. 15:27-28), while remaining acutely aware of human sin.

Saints exhibit the compassion of Christ who wept over the world for failing 'to recognize its time of visitation', i.e., for failing to realize the kingdom of God is just within its reach (cf. Lk. 19:44; 13:34).

Saints are self-possessed, especially in the face of evil. They see evil for what it is - an absence of good. Their grief is a function of their compassion.

Saints know that those who do evil do so because they are deceived. Forgiveness fuels the saint's fortitude in the face of evil.

Saints recognize anger as rooted in grief, and grief as the underside of love. Those possessed of a deified vision see that violence and evil are but disfigured aspirations for God.

Saints know that, at bottom, all desires are desires for Infinite Love. Saints know that sin is always a misguided aspiration for God.

Saints do not lament *diminishment.* They embrace growing old as an image of, and participation in, God's *Ur-kenosis.*[72]

---

[72] See above, n. 12.

Saints inhabit the self-diminishment (*Ur-kenosis*) of God. Abiding in diminishment, they abide in God.

Saints know that Christ is the *self-dispossession* of the Father, and the Spirit is the *self-expropriation* of the Son. Our divinization (*theosis*) is participation in this primordial self-surrender within the Life of the Trinity.

The starving artist is the perfect image of a person who 'is not far from the kingdom of God' (cf. Mk. 12:34). Such persons are possessed of a vision that compels them to 'sell all they have' to 'follow the only light burning in their hearts'.[73]

Saints are possessed of a calling which drives them to transcend normal human needs to pursue their desire for God. They prefer death to an un-deified life.

Saints know they have a specific *mission* in life, even when it is not clearly defined. Saints have no need to be all things to all people. Their only desire is to hold fast to 'the one thing necessary' (cf. Lk. 10:42).

---

[73] 'One dark night, with anxious love inflamed, O, happy lot! Forth unobserved I went … with no other light or guide save that which in my heart was burning' (St. John of the Cross, *Dark Night of the Soul*).

Deified persons are a mixture of self-effacement and self-confidence. They are as unassuming as they can sometimes be overbearing. Always, they are unapologetically themselves.

Theosis strips us of the masks of ego. Saints *glow* with the countenance of Moses who was transfigured when speaking face-to-face with God (cf. Ex. 34:35).

Saints live neither for fame nor fortune. Like all great athletes, they do what they do 'for the love of the game'. They have 'died to themselves' (cf. Lk. 9:24), and 'God lives in them' (cf. Gal. 2:20).

Theosis makes us aware that God is in us *as* us. In deification, we know that 'the Father and I are one' (cf. Jn. 10:30) and that 'the Father is greater than I' (cf. Jn. 14:28).

Saints operate in a sophianic space beyond the comparisons, criticisms, complaints and condemnations of the world. They reflect the smile of the Buddha or the joy of Jesus (cf. Lk. 10:21) whose bliss arises from their immediate experience of God.

Theosis delivers us from the world of rivalry, resentment, rage and retaliation. *Theosis* renders us immune to the contagion of violence.

Deification is caught, not taught. Those anointed by the Spirit of God anoint others with that same Spirit, simply by being themselves.

In his Incarnation, all that Christ has received from his Father is poured out upon the whole of humanity. 'God became man so that man could become God'.[74]

Christ is the Light-become-visible, generated by the Uncreated Light of God (the Father). We are *by participation* what Christ is *by nature:* lights from Light, 'gods in God'.[75]

All things are instantiations of God's creative Light and Love. For those with eyes to see, creation is a *theophany* of God's self-expression.

---

[74] See above, n. 67.
[75] See above, n. 30.

If sin means treating things or persons as objects to be used, *theosis* implies handling everything and everyone with care. Deified persons receive life as a gift, and regard the world as a *sacrament* of God's Love.

We are divinized with the glory of God each moment we consciously experience the transcendental dimension of our existence. Our *capacity for self-transcendence* is the Spirit of God within us, effecting our deification.

Deified persons can say with St. Paul, 'It is no longer I who live, but Christ living within me' (cf. Gal. 2:20). They know that the eye (I) with which they see God is the same eye (I) with which God sees them.[76]

Once we realize that God is in us *as* us, we are glorified in Christ with the same glory Christ shared with the Father from the beginning (cf. Jn. 17:5).

What is the epiphany that separates the saint from the ordinary person? Is it not that deified persons are aware of their co-inherent unity with God? Is it not their sense that 'they and God are one' yet 'God is greater than they' (cf. Jn. 10:30; 14:28)?

---

[76] See above, n. 1.

Saints are aware that God is in them *as* them, yet not identical *with* them. *Theosis* is a continuous intuition that our very existence is an absolutely fortuitous, yet altogether intentional, creative act of God.

Saints exhibit a situational awareness unknown to those who wander around in the dark. Saints give wide berth to those who have not yet awakened from spiritual somnambulance.

The more deified we become, the more we desire to be stripped of excessive baggage. In *theosis*, we yearn to empty ourselves of everything but God.

The asceticism of the saint is a participation in the trinitarian *kenosis* in which Father and Son divest themselves of everything but each other.

Divinized love is devoid of possessiveness. When loved by a living saint, we feel known, recognized, listened to and affirmed, not because of what we have, can or do, but just because we are.

Deified persons love with a trans-personal love. Their love of 'me' is a function of their prior immersion in a Love that makes our encounter something greater, even, than an 'I-thou' experience.

An encounter with a saint is a momentary revelation of the trinitarian 'We'. In *theosis*, 1+1=3.

We are one with that which we seek. We are 'gods in God'.[77] Recognizing our divine pedigree is the 'one thing necessary' to 'love our neighbor as ourselves' (cf. Lk. 10:42; Mt. 19:19).

Saints are allergic to conflict and immune to violence. They flee argumentation like rats a sinking ship. They realize that those who run the rat race, even if they win, remain rats.

Theosis is a proleptic space of divine delight. Those who experience *theosis* discern, in every positive and negative movement of the heart, a desire for, and premonition of, Absolute Goodness, Beauty and Truth. They recognize every desire as a desire for God.

---

[77] See above, n. 30.

Joy is the infallible sign of the deified person. Saints see through the demented logic of the world, having discovered the divinizing *Logos* of God.

Spiritually awake persons have no beef with the world. Because of their deified vision, they grieve for a world that has not 'recognized the time of its own visitation' (cf. Lk. 19:44).

Those who abide in God are allergic to antinomies, arguments and apologetics. Deification renders saints tone-deaf to the world's diatribes, debates and dogmatics.

Genuine self-love is divine, while the pursuit of self-interest is demonic. Who but the prophet, poet or mystic can see that the world's joie-de-vivre is but gallows humor?

Saints, like the flying Wallendas, work without a net. They mount the high-wires of religion and politics, relying on the updraft of God's Spirit to keep them aloft.

Saints exhibit a freedom and spontaneity unknown to those stuck in religious straightjackets. Deified persons scandalize many but are scandalized by none.

There is no storeroom of sagacity from which the saint systematically draws. They are not 'anxious about what they are to say, but say whatever is given them in that hour, knowing it is not they who speak, but the Holy Spirit' (cf. Mk. 13:11).

Saints know that in God 'we live and move and have our being' (cf. Acts 17:28). In all things, deified persons experience the immediate presence of the risen Christ.

Every moment of the deified heart is of God, from God, and oriented towards God. Saints know that every inclination is a yearning for the good - the Absolute Good - which is God.

Saints experience every human desire as a desire for God, made possible by God. Put differently, saints experience human desire as divine desire desiring itself through created means.

Saints discern in all human yearning God's own self-yearning - a perichoretic[78] circulation of Divine Love into which human desires are drawn, purified and perfected.

---

[78] *Perichoresis* – Greek word meaning 'to dance around', and adopted in Christian theology to describe the interpenetrating presence of each Person of the Trinity within each other. The word seeks to express the dynamic, mutually-indwelling

Better to say 'God's desire' or 'God's delight' instead of 'God's Will'. Nothing that God *desires* promises anything other than deified bliss.

God's sole desire is to share his trinitarian joy with his creation. As the ancient proverb has it: 'I said to the almond tree, 'Speak to me of God'...and it blossomed'.[79]

God's greatest joy is to see us happy.[80] *Karma* is God's corrective mercy accommodated to the fragility of the human race.

God never allows suffering except to deliver us into divine bliss. Most of us, it seems, need to get hit in the head with something like a 2x4 to awaken to the joy of the Lord.

Jesus' impatience with our excuses and explanations is actually a revelation of divine empathy. Christ's exasperation with the ways of the world is the flip-side of his passionate desire that 'all persons be saved and come to the knowledge of the truth' (cf. 2 Tim. 1:4).

---

character of the relations within the Trinity, which can then provide insight into the mutual-indwelling character of the relation between Jesus and His people; see John 14: 11; 20; 23.

[79] Nikos Kazantzakis, *Report to Greco.*

[80] So St. Irenaeus: 'The glory of God is the human person fully alive' (*Against Heresies*, IV, 20, 7).

God's Mercy is a divine solvent that loosens and removes every stain of sin. God's Love is a purifying blow torch that melts our egoic lacquer and refurbishes us with divine beauty.

Love is the divine sledge hammer that breaks the chains of our slavery to sin. In the face of love, demons scatter. In the embrace of Divine Love, all sins are dissolved.

Our deification in Christ involves the disappearance of our deliberative (*gnomic*) will.[81] Once divinized by the Spirit, we, like Christ, not only '*do not* sin' but '*cannot* sin' (cf. 1 Jn. 3:9).

Deified by the Spirit, we are one with Christ as Christ is one with God (cf. Jn. 17:21). In *theosis*, we have no need to think; we have only to thank.

Our desire for God is one with God's own desire for us. In loving us, God is loving himself.

When we come before God 'with empty hands',[82] yet open to God's Presence, two things happen: our hearts are purified of sin, then infused with the deifying glory of God.

---

[81] See above, n. 52.
[82] See Henri J. Nouwen, *With Open Hands*.

When emptied of self-interest, we are saturated with divine life. *Theosis* is the purpose for, and perfection of, ascesis and illumination.

Contemplative prayer is like undergoing radiation treatment for cancer: the tumors of sin are dissolved, and we receive a transfusion of divine healing from 'one degree of glory to the next' (cf. 2 Cor. 3:18).

Theosis reveals that we are one with God, yet we are not God. In deification, we participate in the humility of Christ who, 'even though he was in the form of God, did not deem equality with God something to be grasped at' (cf. Php. 2:6-11).

Like Christ, saints can exclaim, 'The Father and I are one' (cf. Jn. 10:30), and 'the Father is greater than I' (cf. Jn. 14:28). Or, like St. Paul, 'It is no longer I who live, but God who lives in me' (cf. Gal. 2:20).

Saints dispense wisdom, not by thinking, but simply by being themselves. Knowledge of God has become second nature to them. They enjoy both a 'natural' and 'transformative' union with God.[83]

---

[83] The distinction between a 'natural' or 'substantial' union with God - which w enjoy by virtue of our creation - and a 'transformative' union of 'likeness' with

There is an exquisite apperception of divine Goodness in the heart of every saint. Saints see nature as graced all the way down.

For those possessed of a deified vision, there is no 'purely natural' world. They behold the world as 'charged with the grandeur of God'.[84]

Only those not yet deified perceive a division between the sacred and the secular. *Theosis* reveals such a dichotomy to be a demonic delusion.

Saints are space-makers - they create a blessed space of Presence where others can be themselves without fear, shame or guilt. *Theosis* generates an attitude of 'let go and let God'.

God - which we enjoy by grace inn Christ - is made by St. John of the Cross (*Ascent to Mt. Carmel*, II, 5. 3): 'God sustains every soul and dwells in it substantially *even though it may be the greatest sinner in the world. This union between God and creatures always exists.* By it he conserves their being so that if the union should end, they would immediately be annihilated and cease to exist. Consequently, in discussing union with God we are not discussing the substantial union that always exists, but the soul's union with and *transformation in God that does not always exist, except when there is likeness of love.* We will call it the union of likeness; and the former, the essential or substantial union' (emphasis added).

[84] Gerard Manley Hopkins, *God's Granduer.*

Saints are aware of how a loving gaze can be perceived as an accusing stare. They know how easily shame can be stirred up by a simple question or glancing look. Hence, they treat all persons with gentleness and respect.

Saints avoid activating comparative and adversarial behaviors in others, especially with questions and expressions that invite a defensive response. Saints constellate a field of blessed acceptance where people intuitively feel welcome.

Deified persons are incapable of mimetic rivalry.[85] Deference to others is their default position. They *defer* to others, not as a co-dependent defense mechanism, but as an instrument of holy communion.

The divinized person goes against the flow. The saint eschews the herd mentality. Abiding in poised self-transcendence, the saint is deified by the Spirit of Peace.

Distance from the crowd is where the divinizing Spirit of God operates. *Diastasis*[86] is the counter-intuitive key to perfect union, both with God and man.

---

[85] See above, n. 22.

[86] *Diastasis* is a key concept in the theological vision of Hans Urs von Balthasar. Drawing from the mystical vision of Adrienne von Speyr, Balthasar says this: 'What

Solitude is the spiritual space of *theosis*. When they pray, deified persons do not 'babble on like the pagans'; instead, they enter into the inner room of their hearts, communing there with the One who sees, and speaks, in silence' (cf. Mt. 6:6-7).

Theosis is a state of virginal openness to God, untouched and untouchable by rivalry or resentment. Deified persons are impervious to envy and imitative violence.

Spiritually self-aware persons apprehend every moment as a revelation of divine glory. For saints, desolations are simply the inverse of consolations, and every consolation is a foretaste of the kingdom of God.

Religious *formation* serves its purpose only when it gives way to spiritual *transformation*. The path from *obedience to* God to *intimacy with* God (*theosis*) is narrow and difficult, and 'few there are who find it' (cf. Mt. 7:14).

---

seems to us to be the sign of separation of Father and Son is precisely the sign of greatest unification'. In the Trinity, intimacy and alterity (diastasis) are directly, not inversely, proportional. See Balthasar's *Theo-Drama: Theological Dramatic Theory V*, 262. Here Balthasar quotes Adrienne von Speyr, *The Gospel of John III*, 358 regarding the importance of *diastasis* as the secret to every form of unity.

The best thing we can do for others is surrender ourselves more completely to God. The deified person is the sole hope of the world.

The contemplative silence of the saints does more to awaken a somnambulant humanity than a cacophony of political speeches.

Our deification in Christ bringing to completion what God himself has begun. God has a greater stake in our *theosis* than have we, given the fact that the purpose of our creation is his glorification in and through us (cf. Eph. 1:4; Jn. 17:22).

God's 'impassibility' is not divine indifference. That which is 'impassible' in God is his desire that divine joy may be in us and our joy be complete (cf. Jn. 15:11; 1 Jn. 1:4).

We wouldn't be summoned to, or capable of, *theosis* if we weren't already somehow 'divine'. It is because we are 'of God' from 'before the foundation of the world' (cf. Eph. 1:4) that makes possible our deification by God in time and space.

Nothing can become, in either potency or act, something it wasn't already in the mind and heart of God. *Theosis* is our *natural* end as the pinnacle of God's creation.

'Supernatural' or 'sanctifying' grace can be nothing more than God bringing to completion what God himself has already begun. Our *theosis* is the triumph of God's salvific will.

Our wills are *naturally* oriented to God, just as creation is *naturally graced* by God. 'Nothing can ever separate us from the love of God made manifest in Christ Jesus' (cf. Rom. 8:39).

The purification of our minds and hearts is an endless process. As the famous hymn says, 'When we've been there ten thousand years...we've no less days to sing God's praise than when we've first begun'.[87]

Nothing we possess is of ourselves. Our very existence is a gift of God. Even our capacity for *theosis* is an act of God's own self-donation.

---

[87] *Amazing Grace.*

If, in *theosis*, we discover 'the pearl of great price' (cf. Mt. 13:46), we also behold an immortal diamond in every person we meet. For those yet unaware of their divine dignity, our only response is, 'But for the grace of God, there go I...'

Spiritual maturity means relaxing into the persons God created us to be. Our lives are 'hidden with Christ in God' (cf. Col. 3:3).

Discovering God's secret name for each of us (cf. Jer. 1:5; Rev. 2:17) is the key to *theosis*.

Becoming little children (cf. Mt. 18:3) is difficult for those who think themselves accomplished in the spiritual life. Rebirth into the world of God depends on dying to every notion of achievement in this world, even that of personal holiness.

Compassion is of God only when it is free of condescension. Patience is divine only when bereft of patronization.

In *theosis*, God dismantles every barrier between 'us' and 'them' and relieves us of self-congratulation.

What do we see when we look in the mirror but layer upon layer of ego cosmetics? How, other than loving ourselves as Christ loves us (cf. Jn. 15:12), can we uncover 'the faces we had before we were born'?[88]

It is God's own self-communication that makes us 'partakers of God's divine nature' (cf. 2 Pt. 1:4). Even our our capacity to say Yes to *theosis* is an extension of God's uncreated graciousness.

Once *theosis* is attained, the darkness within is dissolved. Once a critical mass of human persons recognize their divine origin and destiny, the darkness in the world will be banished.

---

[88] A paraphrase of the Zen koan known as 'Original Face': 'Show me your face before you were born'.

Le Point Vierge

'At the center of our being is a point of pure truth' - *Le Point Vierge* (the Virginal Point) - 'which belongs entirely to God, which is never at our disposal, from which God disposes of our lies, which is inaccessible to the fantasies of our own mind or the brutalities of our own will. This little point of nothingness and of absolute poverty is the pure glory of God in us'.[89]

Le Point Vierge is the deepest, virginal center of our existence where our 'lives are hidden with Christ in God' (cf. Col. 3:3). Abiding with God in *Le Point Vierge*, we partake of God's divinizing Spirit.

Our virginal connection with the Trinity in 'the deepest center'[90] of our souls is eternal and indestructible. Our original, pristine, and perfect identity in God can be neither effaced nor erased by our sins.

---

[89] Thomas Merton, *Conjectures of a Guilty By-Stander*. It is worth nothing that Merton fastened on his concept by reading and corresponding with the Catholic Islamic scholar, Louis Massignon.

[90] St. John of the Cross compares the innermost recesses of the heart to an 'inner wine cellar' where 'I drank of my Beloved...[and] no longer knew anything, and lost the herd which I was following'. He says, 'This wine cellar is the last and most

In the epicenter of our being (*Le Point Vierge*), the effulgence of God's light and the beauty of our creation is forever undiminished.

The heart of a whirling dervish ... the One Point of the Aikido master ... the center of a teeter-totter's fulcrum ... the equipoise of the spinning figure skater ... the apogee of a ballerina on toe: these are images of the contemplative soul, enveloped in a virginal vortex of surrendered self-possession, drawn upwards into deified union with God.

Saints cultivate *inner poverty* as the path to God's kingdom. 'Poverty of spirit' is the portal into the virginal point of our existence where our true self and God are co-inherent (cf. Col. 3:3).

Le Point Vierge is the mystical center of gravity within where we are umbilically connected to our eternal birthing Source. *Le Point Vierge* is where the 'silver cord' (cf. Eccl. 12.1-8) that draws the soul from our body is invisibly anchored.

---

intimate degree of love in which the soul can be placed in this life..[where] the seven gifts of the Holy Spirit are possessed perfectly...[and] [w]hat God communicates to the soul in this intimate union is totally beyond words' (*The Spiritual Canticle*, 26.1-4).

Le Point Vierge is the *indefinable center point* of our lives where we are indissolubly united, yet completely unconfused, with God.

Le Point Vierge is the *virginal* locus of our existence where our true identity, untouched by ego and evil, is married to God. There, even now, we repose in a nuptial union of incomprehensible beauty and bliss.

Le Point Vierge is an *inner trysting place* where God deifies us with his Spirit and makes us 'partakers of his divine nature' (cf. 2 Pt. 1:4). *Le Point Vierge* is the dwelling place of God's Divine *Sophia*.

Le Point Vierge is the *divine wellspring* within from whence both soul and body are continually created and sustained by an unseen Source of Living Water.

Le Point Vierge is the *divine entrée* in the deepest point of our existence through which God dispossesses us of our possessiveness and divinizes us with his Spirit.

Le Point Vierge is the *indefinable center point* of our identity in God which is impervious to the ups and downs of the teeter-totter of our lives.

Le Point Vierge is the invisible, *inner fulcrum* with which Archimedes could actually have moved the world had he known where to look.

An unrestricted and unconditioned desire for goodness, beauty and truth arises unbidden and irrepressible in the virginal point of our being (*Le Point Vierge*) Every heart, at bottom, is perfectly pure and desirous of God.

Abiding in *Le Point Vierge*, we experience a power and a wisdom (*Sophia*) greater than that of which we are naturally capable. *Le Point Vierge* is the sophianic space within which we are deified, and through which divine glory communicates itself to the world.

Every created object has its own center of gravity, as does the cosmos as a whole. Everything is eternally and inseparably anchored in an axial Source outside itself, from which, towards which, and in which it proceeds. This axial access is *Le Point Vierge*.

Living from the deepest center of our being - *Le Point Vierge* - we experience ourselves as connected to everything and everyone with a kindness and consideration that is of God. Descending into the virginal depth of our own existence, we experience a deifying, compassionate self-transcendence.

Original sin is the *hiatus* between our ontological and epistemological identities. Our eternal, inviolate identity in God is discovered in *Le Point Vierge*.

Who we say we are, or who we think we are, is not who God knows us to be (cf. Col. 3:3). Suffering stems from the discrepancy between our ideas of ourselves and the truth of our existence as experienced in *Le Point Vierge*.

Our essential nature is divine bliss. We are ontologically oriented towards ecstasy. 'Salvation' happens when, in *Le Point Vierge*, we experience our 'glorious freedom' as 'the children of God' (cf. Rom. 8:21).

It has pleased God to share the ecstasy of his trinitarian bliss with us (cf. Jn. 17:13). 'The glory of God is the human person fully alive'.[91]

---

[91] See above, n. 80.

Eternal life is an existential apprehension of our divine origin and destiny. Eternal life is being experimentally assumed into 'the Light in which we see light' (cf. Ps. 36:9).

Eternal life is to abide in the pre-apprehension (*Vorgriff*)[92] of God's infinitely creative Love, in which our finite lives *naturally* participate.

Ontologically, we are beings of Light. Like Christ himself, we are 'light from Light' (cf. Eph. 5:8), 'gods in God'.[93]

Once we discover the virginal point of our existence (*Le Point Vierge*) as 'the narrow way' (cf. Mt. 7:14) leading to peace, we stop being accidental tourists and travel in earnest towards the kingdom of God.

For those who have discovered *Le Point Vierge*, all the way to heaven *is* heaven.

---

[92] *Vorgriff* is a term used by Karl Rahner to promote a teleology of knowledge according to which there is presupposed in every human act of knowing the *Vorgriff auf esse* (the 'pre-apprehension of being'), a transcendental awareness of infinite Being (God). *Vorgriff*, Rahner contends, is an *apriori* condition without which no individual act of knowing could occur. In every act of knowing, Rahner says, the individual person, or 'spirit in the world', has already reached out beyond the world and known the metaphysical reality of 'God' as an Infinite Mystery of truth, goodness and beauty.

[93] See above, n. 30.

In the virginal point of our being, we are one with Mary in her Immaculate Conception. Abiding in *Le Point Vierge,* we become God's Immaculate *Re*-conception.

Le Point Vierge is the hidden entrance into the kingdom of God. Failure to recognize our immediate access into God's interior castle[94] is the cause of our suffering.

Le Point Vierge is an indefinable, virginal point of nothingness where our lives and the Life of the Trinity elide. In *Le Point Vierge,* 'we know as we are known' (cf. 1 Cor. 13:12).

Le Point Vierge is the epicenter of our existence - an invisible, stationary still point[95] - around which the chaos of the world whirls. Ensconced in *Le Point Vierge,* we are unmoved by the world's lies.

---

[94] Phrase borrowed from Teresa of Avila's *Interior Castle.*
[95] An image borrowed from T. S. Eliot: 'At the still point of the turning world. Neither flesh nor fleshless; Neither from nor towards; at the still point, there the dance is, But neither arrest nor movement. And do not call it fixity, here past and future are gathered. Neither movement from nor towards, Neither ascent nor decline. Except for the point, the still point, there would be no dance, and there is only the dance' (*Four Quartets*).

The inviolate genome of our eternal destiny is encoded in the epicenter of our existence (*Le Point* Vierge). There, our lives proceed from the Life of God.

In the deepest center of our souls (*Le Point* Vierge) we are created as 'praises of God's divine glory'.[96] More surely than the oak is contained in the acorn, we are destined to be partakers of trinitarian bliss (cf. 2 Pt. 1:4).

Wanderlust is an attempt to discover, through worldly travel, a destination that can be found only in *Le Point Vierge*. An around-the-world cruise will never bring us to this inner Shangri-La.

What is contemplative prayer other than feeling our way into the virginal point of our being (*Le Point Vierge*)? What is centering prayer other than intentionally indwelling the 'deepest center' of our existence, intuitively cultivating our transcendental (and natural) communion with God?

To ascend to God we must first descend into *Le Point Vierge*. There, we enter a 'luminous darkness' where God reveals himself in silence and stillness (cf. Ps. 46:10).

---

[96] A phrase borrowed from Elizabeth of the Trinity who wished to be called 'The Praise of His Glory'.

Sanctity is a matter of relaxing completely, operating deftly from *Le Point Vierge*. Those abiding with the in-dwelling Trinity allow whatever threatens them to crash and burn of its own momentum.

Mystics operate from the virginal point of their being (*Le Point Vierge*). Their minds are perfectly reposed in their spirits, and their spirits perfectly synchronized with their bodies, and their bodies and souls perfectly attuned to the Holy Spirit.

Le Point Vierge is akin to the pure vacuum in which spiritual quantum entanglement is perceived.[97] What appears in this virginal center is inherently unpredictable; yet, whatever arises there does so in a way that reveals an inherent and unbreakable connection with every other particle in the cosmos.

---

[97] *Quantum entanglement* is the phenomenon of a group of sub-atomic particles being generated, interacting, or sharing spatial proximity in such a way that the quantum state of each particle of the group cannot be described independently of the state of the others, including when the particles are separated by a large distance.

PART THREE

ESCHATA

Gelassenheit

The slightest movement of self-transcendence illumines the soul with the Light of God. One moment of *Gelassenheit*[98] redeems a lifetime of illusory, egoic misadventures.

In Presence, we experience *Gelassenheit*. Presence is a space of pure attentiveness, devoid of agenda, filled with Divine *Sophia*.

Spiritual indolence is the enemy of spiritual growth. Complacency is the death of contemplation. *Gelassenheit* is the antidote to both.

Presence means living in the Power of the Now.[99] *Gelassenheit* means letting-go of past and future, and living completely in the present moment.

---

[98] **Gelassenheit** is a German word with multiple meanings: *relinquishment, surrender, abandonment, submission, detachment, letting-go, allowing, acquiescence,* etc. Meister Eckhart's favorite term for *Gelassenheit* is '*releasement*'. See Philip Krill, *Gelassenheit: Day-by-Day with Meister Eckhart.*

[99] A phrase borrowed from the title of Eckhart Tolle's book, *The Power of Now.*

Presence and *Gelassenheit* are Siamese twins who cannot be separated without killing hem both.

The first word of God is *Gelassenheit*: 'Let it be!' In the space of *Gelassenheit* ('letting-be-ness'), the whole of creation is given permission to be exactly what it is.

Gelassenheit is what makes relationship possible. *Gelassenheit* is what makes communion attainable. *Gelassenheit* is what makes intimacy ecstatic.

Absence is but another form of *Presence*. 'Absence makes the heart grow fonder' because it creates the space of *Gelassenheit* in which the beloved appears ever more beautiful.

Letting go is the key to staying together. *Surrender* is the way to victory in every battle. *Gelassenheit* is the counter-intuitive way of achieving everything our hearts desire.

Gelassenheit is the mystical water dissolving every resistance, wearing down every rough edge. Letting go of all judgments and resentments is the best way of being available - and invaluable - to others.

God is a triune Mystery of *Gelassenheit* (letting-go-ness). God is an *Ur-kenosis* of self-surrendering Love.[100] God's inherent self-relinquishment (*Gelassenheit*) results in the Big Bang of creation.

As in the *Gelassenheit* of God, so too in human life: every act of *intentional surrender* produces an unimaginable *excess* of divine abundance.

Gelassenheit is a theophanic manifestation of God as Pure Act (*Actus Purus*).[101] Like God, *Gelassenheit* is the actualization of personal potential without remainder.

Deification occurs when we acquire a continuous disposition of *Gelassenheit*. Practicing *Gelassenheit*, we become by grace what God is by nature.

The power of *Presence* (*Gelassenheit*) is stronger than the generations of blood-lust which is humanity's sinful pedigree. One moment of *Gelassenheit* opens the kingdom of God to the most hardened heart (cf. Lk. 23:43).

---

[100] See above, n. 12.
[101] See n. 2, 11.

Gelassenheit is to become as nothing so that others, in our *presence*, can discover their true worth. *Gelassenheit* is that mystical space, devoid of judgment, where others discover themselves to be loved by God.

Gelassenheit is an act of divine *kenosis*. *Gelassenheit* of empties us of self-interest, creating a space for connection to occur. *Gelassenheit* is a participation in the peace of God.

Gelassenheit is the spiritual glue that holds sin and grace together. Letting go of critical judgments, we become *compassionately aware* - without accusation or condemnation - of the character defects of ourselves and others.

Awareness of our sins is simultaneously their redemption. *Gelassenheit* enables a divine self-transcendence that dispossesses us of our possessiveness.

Gelassenheit is our exit ramp from the highway to hell. In *Gelassenheit*, God transports us from the suffering of our sins into the joy of God's Embrace.

For those awakened to the redemptive force of *Gelassenheit*, the need for discipline is replaced by the delight of doing what's right. For those who know the bliss of Presence, virtue is their natural *élan*.

What is it about a Japanese tea ceremony that touches us so? What is it about a whirling dervish that moves the soul? Is it not an intuitive awareness that one moment of pure *Presence* (*Gelassenheit*) is more powerful than all the world's sound and fury?

What we are looking for in beauty is found most perfectly in *Presence*. *Gelassenheit* (the practice of letting-go) is the transformative space in which erotic fascination becomes blissful appreciation.

Those who abide in *Gelassenheit* have the time of their lives at every moment. In *Gelassenheit*, every *Now* is an epiphany of God's glory.

In *Gelassenheit*, we experience our intrinsic connection with God. In *Gelassenheit*, we look upon the world with an acutely observing mind, backlit with compassion.

It is the machinations of our minds that obscure a deified vision. *Gelassenheit* is the space of attentive docility where God manifests his transcendent *Presence*.

Gelassenheit allows us to 'stand outside ourselves', seeing ourselves and others as 'unprofitable servants' (cf. Lk. 17:10). In *Gelassenheit,* we find the grace to say, 'Father, forgive us, for we do not know what we are doing' (cf. Lk. 23:34).

Gelassenheit allows us to receive the self-disclosure of others without distortions, judgment, envy or fear. Spiritual maturity is learning how to abide in this forgiving space of letting-go.

Fully surrendered persons live fully in the present moment. Their's is the world of *Gelassenheit.* They have discovered 'the kingdom of God within' (cf. Lk. 17:21).

Those who experience divine releasement'[102] (*Gelassenheit*) are astounded by the '*is-ing-ness*' of things. They are enraptured by their 'intuition of being'.[103]

---

[102] See above, n. 98.
[103] See above, n. 11.

In *Gelassenheit,* we catch a glimpse of the fortuity of creation. *Gelassenheit* is the 'holy ground' (cf. Ex. 3:5; Acts 7:33) where the world reveals itself as theophanic.

In the world of *Gelassenheit,* everything is eternally fresh and perfect. Abiding there, it's as if we are continually witnessing the first moments of creation.

Every moment spent in 'divine relinquishment' (*Gelassenheit*) instantly ushers us into the kingdom of God. One moment of loving surrender (*Gelassenheit*) overcomes a lifetime of darkness.

Bottomless is the epicenter of divine relinquishment. Plunging into the infinite depths of our graced nothingness in *Gelassenheit,* we ascend into ever-increasing, eternal bliss.

Every moment is pregnant with a proleptic taste of eternity. Feeling the power of the present moment (*Gelassenheit*), we have found the 'narrow way' into the kingdom of God (cf. Mt. 7:14).

Francis of Assisi once remarked that true joy is knocking at the door of one's own monastery and being unrecognized and rejected. For those who know the power of *Gelassenheit*, even vilification is cause for rejoicing.

Gelassenheit allows us to recognize disappointment as an invitation from God to surrender more completely into his Divine Embrace. Suffering becomes *redemptive* only in the space of *Gelassenheit*.

Gelassenheit is 'delightful detachment'. Joyous surrender *compels* God to divinize us, since *Gelassenheit* is a participation in God's own *Ur-kenosis* (self-surrender).[104]

The dying of the light on an autumn afternoon unveils a delicate beauty - a beauty intuitively more real than death itself. This beauty is *Gelassenheit*.

Love, experienced in *Gelassenheit*, is the death of death. 'Perfect love casts out all fear', especially the 'fear of death' (cf. 1 Jn. 1:5; Heb. 2:15).

---

[104] See above, n. 12.

Death is the *form* of life, just as the soul is the *form* of the body.[105] Christ rose from the dead the *moment* he embraced his coming death (cf. Lk. 22:42).

Christ's act of *Gelassenheit* when embracing his cross is the redemption of the cosmos. It's not Christ's *agony* that is redemptive, but his joyous acceptance (*Gelassenheit*) (cf. Heb. 2:2).

Either death has the final word or it does not. Otherwise why would Christ have said, 'No greater love has anyone than that they lay down their life for another' (cf. Jn. 15:13)? In *Gelassenheit*, self-surrender is revealed as salvation.

Why do we call those who risk their lives as first responders 'heroes', if not because we recognize the death-transcending power of their self-sacrificial love (*Gelassenheit*)?

Blessed are they who, after a lifetime of accolades and accomplishments, come to regard their autobiography as 'chronicles of wasted time'.[106]

---

[105] *Form* here mens 'the inner nature' or 'ontological structure' of things.
[106] Malcom Muggeridge, *Chronicles of Wasted Time: An Autobiography*.

Blessed are they who cherish *disillusionment* as the door to the kingdom of God.

Blessed are they who, by cultivating *Gelassenheit*, have risen from death of the ego into the realm of the Spirit.

Failure is the unavoidable path to forgiveness. *Gelassenheit* is the indispensable path to glory.

Death of the *persona* is the precondition for awakening to God. *Gelassenheit* is the antidote to greed and self-glorification (cf. Lk. 16:13).

'You have died and your life is hidden with Christ in God' (cf. Col. 3:3). Sanctity is a 'living death', i.e., an unceasing act of *Gelassenheit* (letting-go-ness).

Wisdom is recognizing *Gelassenheit* as God's deifying self-communication.

Apokatastasis

Apokatastasis[107] must be the truth of the gospel if the deification of humanity is the purpose of the Incarnation.[108]

Only *Apokatastasis* does justice to both God's desire (cf. 2 Tim. 1:4) and ability (cf. Job 42:2; Eph. 1:11) to save all.

How can the gospel be good news if *any* of God's children are lost forever? The *kerygma*[109] is an insult to God when reduced to: 'Be good or you might not get into heaven'.

How we do anything is how we do everything. If one person doesn't matter, nobody matters. These are the non-theological reasons why *Apokatastasis* must be true of the all-merciful God (cf. Isa. 49:15; Jn. 6:39).

---

[107] ***Apokatastasis*** – Greek term referring to 'restoration'. In colloquial use, *Apokatastasis* refers to 'universal salvation'. This 'restoration of all things' is picked up and used among Patristic Era theologians in a speculative way regarding God's eschatological intentions for all creation, including all which was 'lost' through the Fall.
[108] See above, n. 67.
[109] See above, n. 24.

What does it mean to say God's love is 'unconditional' if we don't really mean it? Failing *Apokatastasis*, every 'theology of hope' has a false bottom.

If all persons will be saved, what about sin and evil? St. Irenaeus answers: 'Since he who saves always existed, it was necessary that those who would need to be saved should be created, so that he who saves should not exist in vain'.[110]

Shouldn't the burden of proof be on those who resist *Apokatastasis* rather than upon those who propose it as a *theologumenon*?[111] How can *Apokatastasis* not be true if we are inextinguishably and transcendentally oriented to perfect union with God?

Because of our absolute and ineradicable draw towards God (cf. Jn. 12:32), we are, as it were, 'doomed to happiness'.[112] Hell, as a 'place of conscious, eternal torment', is incompatible with our ontological orientation to divine bliss.

---

[110] A paraphrase of St. Irenaeus, *Against Heresies*, 3.22.3, quoted in John Behr, *The Mystery of Christ: Life in Death*, 77.

[111] A *theologumenon* is an exercise in theological imagination. It is a theological statement which is an individual opinion, not a question of doctrine.

[112] David Bentley Hart, *That All Shall Be Saved*, 40-41.

If the Glad Tidings of the risen Christ are true, it is disingenuous for Christians to doubt *Apokatastasis*. Either Christ has *definitively* triumph over sin, death and evil, or he has not.

The gospel of the risen and triumphant Christ implies a final *Apokatastasis* in which all things are redeemed and joined to God (cf. 1 Cor. 15:28). How can God be 'all in all' (cf. 1 Cor. 15:28-29) if some are left behind?

The *kerygma* of the first witnesses to the risen Christ is incoherent if it does not imply the recapitulation and redemption of the entirety of creation. Christ has reconciled *all things* in himself (cf. Col. 1:20; 1 Cor. 15:27).

It is the gospel itself that is responsible for the deconstruction of institutionalized Christianity.[113] The promissory vision of *Apokatastasis* is both the cause and cure of religious indifference.

If *Apokatastasis* is not irrefutably true - both logically and theologically - the *kerygma* is nothing other than Law writ large.

---

[113] On the deconstruction of the institutional church, see Bradley Jersak, *Out of the Embers: Faith After the Great Deconstruction.*

The glad tidings of the gospel (cf. Isa. 45:23; Rom. 14:11; Php. 2:10) are predicated on *Apokatastasis* as the fullest revelation of God's eternal identity.

Apokatastasis is the necessary flip side of creation *ex nihilo*. The gratuity of God's creative Word in creation is mirrored and completed in the restitution of all things in Christ.

In God, protology and eschatology are synonymous.[114] Christ is the *Alpha* and *Omega* (cf. Rev. 1:8). *Apokatastasis* is the cosmic Christ (*Totus Christus*) 'come to full stature' (cf. Eph. 4:13).

Apokatastasis leaves many pious believers incredulous. Could this be because 'we are envious that God is so generous' (cf. Mt. 20:15; Rom. 9:14-16)?

The gospel of Christ has been rejected, not because it is too hard, but because it's too good to be true. 'He came to his own and his own received him not, but to everyone who did receive him, he gave the power to become the children of God' (cf. Jn. 1:12). Our resistance to *Apokatastasis* may be more a commentary on our lack of faith than on God's desire to give us more than we deserve (cf. 1 Jn. 4:10; 1 Cor. 4:7).

---

[114] **Protology** refers to God's act of creation, **eschatology** to God's act of cosmic redemption.

If we had a more vibrant 'eschatological imagination',[115] *Apokatastasis* would seem just another undeniable dimension of God's ever-greater glory.

If we learned to read the Scriptures backwards,[116] *Apokatastasis* would be the *starting point* for our contemplation of the drama of salvation. Such a narrative would be shot through, from beginning to end, with an undying light of eternal promise.

For those possessed of an anagogical vision, *Apokatastasis* is the culmination of the Paschal Mystery. It represents the completion of Christ's Ascension in which he 'lifts up all things to himself' (cf. Jn. 12:32).

The Immaculate Conception and Glorious Assumption of the Blessed Virgin Mary illumine our belief in *Apokatastasis*. If Mary is redeemed from all sin by the grace of her Son, why should we not believe that he can, and will, do the same for everyone?

---

[115] A phrase borrowed from the works of James Alison. See his *Raising Abel: The Recovery of the Eschatological Imagination* and *Living in the End Times: The Last Things Reimagined.*
[116] See Richard B. Hays, *Reading Backwards: Figural Christology and the Fourfold Gospel Witness.*

Failing *Apokatastasis*, the God we believe in seems no more worthy of our love than a cat playing with a mouse.

How can the God who creates *ex nihilo* in utter gratuity from an uncontainable effulgence of Divine Love do so with the purpose of discarding part of his creation at the end?

Did not the God of infinite grace create the cosmos for no other purpose than to infuse it with his own why-less joy?

Our hope for *Apokatastasis* is an intuitive apprehension of God's insatiable desire to share Himself with those made in his own image and likeness (cf. Gen. 1:26). Without this intuition, the *kerygma* of Christ is as incoherent as it is anodyne.

Apokatastasis affirms the absolute fortuity of the One who creates *ex nihilo*. Nothing is created from nothing to become nothing again. God creates only to glorify that which God has made.

Apokatastasis is the fitting eschatological complement to the inexplicably beneficent act of God's act of creation. Otherwise, God is either schizophrenic or Manichean.[117]

---

[117] See above, n. 55.

Apokatastasis affirms the pre-eternal unity of humanity with divinity in Christ. *Apokatastasis* reveals the fullness of what God has envisioned 'before the foundation of the world' (cf. Eph. 1:4).

Humanity is hardwired for communion with the tri-personal Source of its own hardwiring. *Apokatastasis* is the only coherent, finally satisfactory *telos* of our insatiable desire for God.

Our infinite and insatiable desire for God is the unconditioned Presence of God within us. *Apokatastasis* affirms that God's desire for creatures is unconditionally benevolent.

Every creature's final *end* determines the form of its beginning. How can our final destiny be anything less glorious than *Apokatastasis* if our creation by God was an unconditioned act of pure love?

If *Apokatastasis* is not true, how is the gospel not a tawdry tale of human tragedy? How is the gospel a 'gospel of joy'[118] if God's solution to the problem of evil is to 'do unto us as we have done unto others'?

---

[118] See Pope Francis, *The Joy of the Gospel (Evangelii Gaudium)*.

Apokatastasis envisions God as 'all in all' (cf. 1 Cor. 15:28). Despite our sins, we are destined, 'with unveiled faces, to behold the majesty of the Lord, 'changed from one degree of glory to another' (cf. 2 Cor. 3:18).

If *Apokatastasis* is not the final end of history, what could the purpose of creation be other than to be 'sound and fury signifying nothing'?[119] Is the God of the gospel the religious equivalent of Macbeth?

No one can be argued into believing in *Apokatastasis*. Confident universalism is an intuitive, anagogical apprehension of God's grand, glorious plan for humanity, based on our God-given, ineluctable orientation to God.

Failing a belief in *Apokatastasis*, is it any wonder that institutional Christianity has proven itself incapable of proclaiming the *kerygma* with the convincing power of those first witnesses of the resurrection?

---

[119] See above, n. 67.

The whole of creation, from the smallest, sub-atomic particle to the whole of the ever-expanding cosmos, is inherently relational, grounded as it is in the trinitarian relationality of God. In the Total Christ (*Totus Christus*), the whole of the cosmos is redeemed and glorified by the One who created it.

If Christ is the *Alpha* and *Omega* of creation, how can 'the completion of all things in Christ' (cf. Col. 1:17-20) not equate to *Apokatastasis*?

If Christ is the Eternal Word 'through and for whom all things are made' (cf. Col. 1:16), then creation is Incarnation and Christology is cosmology.[120]

How can resistance to the notion of *Apokatastasis* stem from anything other than a desire to disbelieve either God's omnipotence or doubt God's benevolence?

Apokatastasis reveals what mystics of every generation have known: that God's desire for eternal and indivisible union with humanity is both greater than, and the Source of, our desire to live with God forever (cf. Lk. 12:32).

---

[120] This was the *theologumenon* of St. Maximus the Confessor. See Jordan Daniel Wood, *The Whole Mystery of Christ: Creation as Incarnation in Maximus the Confessor.*

If God '*desires* that all be saved and come to a knowledge of his truth' (cf. 2 Tim. 1:40), but *cannot* make it happen, how can God be *omnipotent*? If God is *able* to save all (cf. Lk:37) but *decides not to do so*, how can God be *benevolent*? If God is *neither able nor willing* to save all, then why call him 'God'?[121]

What if the '*Last*' Judgment means just that, i.e., 'the *termination*' of all judgment' (cf. Jn. 3:17; 5:22; 1 Cor. 2:15)? Isn't this the promise of *Apokatastasis*?

Hope of *Apokatastasis* is tacitly affirmed by those who deny it in the same way that God is implicitly affirmed by the atheist. Unless insane, those who deny *Apokatastasis* nevertheless *wish* it were true.

If every person is ontologically oriented in love towards God, how is it possible that any person would not share in the inconceivable bliss God promises to 'those who love him' (cf. 1 Cor. 2:9)?

---

[121] A paraphrase of the famous quote from Epicurus: 'Is God willing to prevent evil, but not able? Then he is not omnipotent. Is he able, but not willing? Then he is malevolent. Is he both able and willing? Then whence cometh evil? Is he neither able nor willing? Then why call him God?'

If our desire for the Good, the True and the Beautiful comes from God - and indeed is the very Life of God within us - how can it lead us anywhere but into God?

How could any rational creature fail to reach the end for which God Himself has created us? And how could our arrival at our glorious destination be anything other than participation in God's own perfect bliss (*Apokatastasis*)?

What would happen if our scriptural and philosophical assertions about the 'wrath of God' or 'divine justice' were viewed in a restorative instead of a retributive key? Would not our openness to *Apokatastasis* expand to match the infinite 'depth and breadth' of God's mercy itself (cf. Eph. 3:18; Mt. 5:45)?

God's presumed willingness to exclude even a single person from *Apokatastasis* implies that he is quite prepared to lose *all* those his Son was sent to save (cf. Ezk. 34:16; Jn. 6:39). How is this logic of 'acceptable risk' not the opposite of Jesus' proclamation, 'I have come to seek and save that which is lost' (cf. Lk. 19:10)?

Our capacity to do evil could never be greater than God's capacity to show Mercy. Where, then, do we get the idea that our ability to commit sin meriting eternal torment, is stronger than God's capacity to effect a blessed *Apokatastasis*?

Consigning someone to eternal torment for their sins, regardless of kind and number, is as ignorant for condemning a 65-year old woman for not bearing more children.

If 'apart from God we can do nothing' (cf. Jn. 15:5), God would be condemning himself when sending anyone to hell.

The 'fires of hell' are identical with the 'consuming fire' (cf. Heb. 12:29) of God's Mercy.[122] Divine justice and Divine Mercy are a single Mystery of God's incandescent, glorious Love, burning away the impurity of our sins so that we ourselves *may be saved* (cf. 1 Cor. 3:15).

The insistence on hell as a place of eternal, intentional torment is nothing other than a narcissistic inversion of *Apokatastasis* for the dourly disposed.

---

[122] See George MacDonald's famous sermon, '*The Consuming Fire*' in *Unspoken Sermons*.

By God's grace, we can be no more impeded from reaching our final destiny in God (*Apokatastasis*) than could the Magi from reaching Bethlehem. By God's grace, our sins are no more an impediment to salvation than were the evil designs of Herod.

'The Word of God wills that the Mystery of his Incarnation be actualized always and in all things'.[123] *Apokatastasis* is the anagogical expression of this pre-eternal truth.

Apokatastasis is the incredulous affirmation of St. Paul's counter-intuitive assertion that 'God has consigned all men to disobedience, that he may have mercy upon all' (cf. Rom. 11:32).

St. Thomas Aquinas, following St. Augustine, tells us that it is impossible for any rational creature to intentionally choose to do evil.[124] *Apokatastasis* is the theological confirmation of this metaphysical intuition.

Christ promised to 'draw all things to himself' (cf. Jn. 12:32), including the criminal crucified next to him (cf. Lk. 23:43). In the light of these words, *Apokatastasis* appears as the fulfillment of all desire, both human and divine.

---

[123] St. Maximus the Confessor, *Ambigua*, 7, 22, cited in Daniel Jordan Wood, *ibid.*
[124] See above, n. 53.

Apokatastasis is the singular purpose of our creation. Protology and eschatology are identical in God.[125] God's final desire for our lives is participation in His anagogical *Plērōma* (cf. 1 Cor. 15:28; Eph. 1:23; 4:6).

Apokatastasis is more a divine design than a human desire. God's glorification of humanity in *Apokatastasis* is God's glorification of himself, in which we are blessed to participate.

No one goes to heaven without passing through hell. *Apokatastasis* affirms that it is the very *Excess* of God's Uncreated Light and Love that causes us, upon death, to experience a hellish period of acclimation to divine bliss.

Apokatastasis is neither cheap grace, nor the avoidance of judgment. Hell is the inevitable precondition for *Apokatastasis*.

The blinding, Uncreated Light of God (cf. 1 Jn. 1:5) 'punishes' and 'banishes' all darkness occluding the human psyche before acclimating it to heavenly bliss.

---

[125] See above, n. 114.

The eschatological 'punishment' of God can be likened to that of concentration camp victims attempting to ingest the foods delivered by their liberating Allies. It is the very *richness* of God's unconditional love that makes those who have never tasted such fare sick to their stomachs.

Apokatastasis is synonymous with the 'Wedding Feast of the Lamb' (cf. Rev. 19:9), where a world that has traded its birthright for a 'bowl of gruel' (cf. Gen. 25:33) will dine on rich foods and fine wines' of God's kingdom (cf. Isa. 25:6).

How can grace be grace if it could ever be lost? If our very existence is a grace, how could our final End be anything less than a grace-filled *Apokatastasis*?

When the risen Christ manifested himself to St. Paul on the road to Damascus (Acts 9), Saul's previous religious certainties dissolved like the morning mist. *Apokatastasis* affirms that something similar occurs for the whole world when Christ comes again.

Would not the unveiling of the glorified Christ so *relativize* our conceptions of God, ourselves and the world as to make us 'new creations in Christ' (cf. 2 Cor. 5:17)? How could it be otherwise if God's desire is never to destroy but always to redeem (cf. Ezek. 18:23, 32; Jn. 3:17; 12:47; Lk. 19:19)?

Would not the second coming of Christ bring such incomprehensible Light and Joy as to dispel every conceivable shadow of fear, doubt, and sin? How could the shadows of our moral lacunae defeat the unconquerable Light of the risen Lord?

The terror and dread of the *Apocalypse* must necessarily resolve themselves into the bliss and relief of *Apokatastasis*. Otherwise God's judgment is vindictive, not redemptive, and God's mercy is, at bottom, mendacious.

Since all things, from their very beginning, 'live and move and have their being' in God (cf. Acts 17:28), how could nature and history culminate in anything other than *Apokatastasis*?

If the *Shalom* (Peace) of God is synonymous with the *Shekinah* (Presence)[126] of God, how could anyone experience the all-redeeming power of God's Presence without also believing *Apokatastasis* to be the final Peace of God?

---

[126] *Shekinah* is a visible manifestation of God on earth, whose presence is portrayed through a natural occurrence. The word *Shekinah* is a Hebrew name meaning 'dwelling' or 'one who dwells'. *Shekinah* means 'He caused to dwell', referring to the divine *Presence* of God. See Ex. 25:22; Lev. 16:2; 2 Sam. 6:2; 2 Kin. 19:14, 15; Psa. 80:1; Isa. 37:16; Ezek. 9:3; 10:18; Heb. 9:5.

God works within us 'both to will and to work for his good pleasure' (Phil. 2:13). Why, then, would God condemn us when we fail to achieve what only His working can accomplish?

Failing *Apokatastasis*, would not God only be condemning Himself, since all things abide in God (cf. Col. 1:17)?

How can we stand before God and be condemned for having empty hands when we have nothing of our own to begin with (cf. Jn. 15:5)? What sort of God would it be who judges us harshly for not having what he himself has not given?

Apokatastasis invites us to imagine God as no less gracious that we who are evil (cf. Mt. 7:11). If God is not more understanding than 'the unjust judge' (cf. Lk. 16:6-8) or the 'good enough parent',[127] why bother?

Would loving parents promise a great Christmas present to their child, then wait to see if the child is able to find it? Would loving parents promise a fabulous birthday gift to their child, yet withhold the gift if the child could not unwrap it?

---

[127] Phrase borrowed from the title of Bruno Bettelheim's book, *A Good Enough Parent: A Book on Child-Rearing.*

How can the *kerygma* be good news at all if not backlit by the golden light of the *Apokatastasis*? What is the joy of the gospel if not that all of humanity will be assimilated, by God's grace, into a final consummation of divine glory?

We can know neither ourselves nor others as we are known by God (cf. 1 Cor. 13:12). Judgment of others has no place in those who abide in God, just as there is no judgement in God himself (cf. Mt. 7:1; Jn. 8:15).

The temples of the Janus-faced God are empty. The Dr. Jekyll-Mr.Hyde God of the churches no longer convinces. The world is beginning to awaken to the reality that 'the Father's sun shines on the good and bad alike, and his rain falls upon the just and the unjust' (cf. Mt. 5:45).

We are the subjects and benefactors of a divine alchemy. God takes each of our leaden hearts, works his magic, then, presto!, God has turned lead into gold (cf. Isa. 1:18).

The slightest glimpse of created beauty is an epiphany of God's infinite glory. An entire life of crime is redeemed with the briefest flash of theophanic light.

It was the risen Christ's most heavenly joy to descend into hell. There, he was pleased to 'set the captives free' (cf. Lk. 4:18).

In his 'harrowing of hell', Christ has rescued those the world has discarded, discredited, disowned and damned.

How can Christ, now that he is 'lifted up' and 'seated at the right hand of the Father' (cf. Lk. 22:69; Eph. 2:6; Col. 3:1), fail, in any measure, to 'draw all things to himself' (cf. Jn. 8:32)?

If Christ is to 'deliver the kingdom to God the Father after destroying every rule and every authority and power' (cf. 1 Cor. 15:24-29), how can anyone be left behind?

Plērōma

'All will be well, and all manner of things will be well'.[128]

To the degree we are rendered incredulous by the prospect of universal salvation, we are blinded by our sins. In the *Plērōma,* God's desire that 'all be saved and come to a knowledge of the truth' (cf. 2 Tim. 1:4) is fulfilled.

In the *Plērōma,* God, in Christ, 'reconciles all things in himself' (cf. Col. 1:20).

Forgiveness has no place in God, since, in God, there is nothing to forgive. The Persons of the Trinity *give* everything *for* the Other, finding in the Other nothing to forgive.

To understand completely is to forgive completely. If we could see with the eyes of God, we would remain mute before the misdeeds of others.

---

[128] See above, n. 44.

When everything is understood, everything is joyfully accepted. To have the 'mind of Christ' (cf. 1 Cor. 2:16), is to see that God's timing is always perfect, and that nothing is not wonderfully redeemed in the *Plērōma*[129] of God's recreative Love.

'Mercy' is Divine Love as seen through human sin. 'Mercy' is what *we* ask for when we have not grasped the inexorable and all-redeeming Love of God.

Purpose precedes production. Just as Michelangelo envisioned his statue of David before he set upon his block of marble, so did God envision all things reconciled in Christ before he created the world (cf. Col. 1:16-20).

Christ 'come to full stature' (cf. Eph. 4:13) is identical with God's Eternal Word. The Total Christ (*Totus Christus*) of God's *Plērōma* is also the One 'through whom and for whom all things were made', and in whom 'all things hold together' (cf. Col. 1:15-17).

---

[129] *Plērōma* is a Greek word translated 'fullness', or 'totality'. In Scripture, it refers to the fullness of God in Christ and the recapitulation and redemption of all things in Christ.

The End is in the beginning, and the beginning makes sense only in light of the End.

Christ is the *Omega* of God's redemptive plan before he is the *Alpha* of all creation.

Our eternal destiny in God's blissful *Plērōma* is the 'reason' it has pleased God to create us (and everything else) from the beginning.

Once we see that God is, and will be, 'all in all' (cf. 1 Cor. 15:28), we glimpse a Love that 'no eye has seen, nor ear heard, nor any human mind has fully comprehended' (cf. 1 Cor. 2:9).

Captured by a vision of God's *Plērōma*, we experience a joy and a peace the world cannot give (cf. Jn. 14:27).

All things are created for, and ontologically attuned to, a final recapitulation (*Plērōma*) in Christ (cf. Eph. 1:10). The *Totus Christus* (Total Christ) is the divine terminus of the God's cosmos.

As humanly divine creatures, we are privileged to perceive the teleological structure of reality, abiding in the bliss given to those who recognize the divine inscape[130] of creation.

Nothing in this world is self-explanatory. Even organic, vegetative and animal life forms exhibit patterns of complexification and unification that portend a Final *Plērōma*.

God's predestined *Plērōma* is what accounts for the purposeful patterns of the universe. Creation is what it is only because of what it will become.

There is no scientific answer to the perennial philosophical question: 'Why is there something rather than nothing'. Only a vision of an all-perfecting *Plērōma* accounts the infinite forms of being, each hard-wired with its own *entelechy*.[131]

God's purpose, both in our creation and in our purgation, is to make us partakers of his *Plērōma* (cf. 2 Pt. 1:4). We are chosen in Christ 'before the foundation of the world' (cf. Eph. 1:4) so that his 'joy may be in us and our joy be complete' (cf. Jn. 15:11).

---

[130] 'Inscape' ('intrinsic beauty') is a mystical notion promoted by the poet, Gerard Manley Hopkins, patterned on the mystical theology of John Duns Scotus.
[131] See above, n. 42.

To love a world steeped in sin, we must *intuit* our originalperfection in the eschatological purposes of God. Christian love is not possible without an anagogical vision of our eternal identity in God (cf. Jer. 1:5), and of our predestined place in God's final *Plērōma*.

Nothing can come from God and return to God without fulfilling the purpose for which God called it into being (cf. Isa. 55:11). Our imperfections, failures and sins are nothing but raw material for God's act of eschatological *kintsugi*.[132]

Christ's love for the poor, the unclean, and the socially-radioactive stems from his immediate apprehension of his Father as the beloved Creator and Redeemer of all. Christ sees and loves us as God's perfect children, destined for eternal joy (cf. Lk. 12:32).[133]

Like God, Christ sees beneath the surface of our sins and loves us as the persons he created us to be. Further, God creates nothing that does not return to him, having fulfilled the glorious purpose for which he conceived it (cf. Isa. 55:10-11).

---

[132] Kintsugi is the Japanese art of repairing broken pottery by mending the areas of breakage with lacquer dusted or mixed with powdered gold, silver or platinum. *Kintsugi* treats breakage and repair as part of the history of an object, rather than something to disguise.

[133] See Alvin F. Kimel, *Destined for Joy: The Gospel of Universal Salvation.*

Unless we begin with the End in mind, we understand nothing. An acorn is only a nut until the oak is envisioned. A sinner is only a sinner until the reconciliation of all things in Christ is seen (cf. 2 Cor. 1:19).

Despair is a logical choice only until we glimpse our predestined glorification in Christ (cf. Jn. 17:22). An eschatological vision of God's *Plērōma* banishes the darkness of doubt and depression.

What choice do we have when God's Truth hits us full in the face? The truth of God's Love is at once indicting and disarming, convicting and liberating. Face-to-face with God, all we can do is remain blissfully silent (cf. Rev. 8:1).

There is no one languishing in hell who, through sheer suffering and exasperation, will not discover despair as the door to a final surrender leading to freedom. The *Plērōma* of Infinite Love outlasts and overcomes all human obstreperousness.

Love conquers all. Divine Love is an infinite ocean of Acceptance where our resentments go to drown. God is a *Plērōma* of Divine Mercy in which the world's pretense dissolves like the sunken Titanic.

God's compassion *is* God's judgement. The so-called 'last judgement' is exactly that: the end of all judgement in the Light of God's *Plērōma*

There is nowhere we can flee that the Hound of Heaven[134] has not already gone before us. In all things, God works for the glorification of all his creatures.

In the *Plērōma*, the whole and the part, the one and the many, mutually affirm and condition each other. Union differentiates, and perfect union differentiates perfectly.[135]

Nothing is ever lost in the economy of God. The interchangeability of matter and energy is a cosmic reflection of God's all-redemptive love.

We become at once infinitely compassionate and deeply grieved when we observe a world unaware of its own self-transcendence. Failing a vision of the *Plērōma* (i.e. the reconciliation of all things in Christ), there is no good news gospel (cf. Col. 1:20).

---

[134] The title of a poem by Francis Thompson.
[135] Phrase attributed, without specific reference in his writings, to Pierre Teilhard de Chardin. See: '*You Are Not a Human Being Having a Spiritual Experience. You Are a Spiritual Being Having a Human Experience*' – Quote Investigator®. 20 June 2019, quoteinvestigator.com/2019/06/20/spiritual.

God is in a non-competitive, co-inherent relationship with everything God has created. God is an infinite ocean of mercy in which currents of divine grief merge into a *Plērōma* of divine glory.

Any vision of God that does not begin and end with the *Plērōma* is blasphemy. God frightens us only to set us free from our 'slavery to sin' (cf. Rom. 6:18).

Nothing compelled is of God, though an experience of the goodness of God compels fidelity. Religionists could learn a thing or two from *Alcoholics Anonymous* whose public relations policy is 'based on attraction, not promotion'.

Religion is a cocoon of deception necessary for some human butterflies before they can spiritually fly. Piety is an impoverished surrogate for an inspiring vision of the *Plērōma*.

'The Word of God, very God, wills always and in all things to actualize the mystery of his Incarnation'.[136] The *Plērōma* is the fulfillment of Christ's promise that 'when I am lifted up I will draw all things to myself' (cf. Jn. 12:32).

---

[136] St. Maximus the Confessor, *Ambigua* 7.22.

Only the anagogical Light of God's final *Plērōma* can transform horror into humor, blight into beatitude. Evil and death are the defining limits of our vision until our eschatological imagination equals that of St. Paul.

How can the 'real distinction'[137] between the Creator and creation not find its teleological fulfillment in the *Plērōma*?

If all comes from God (cf. Jn. 1:3), and God is Love (cf. 1 Jn. 4:5-8), must not all return to God (cf. Col. 1:17; Eph., 1:22; 1 Cor,. 15:25-27) in a *Plērōma* of infinite bliss (cf. Jn. 1:16; Eph. 1:10)?

The unexpected bliss of the *Plērōma* is the eschatological flip-side of God's unconditionally beneficent act of creation. The *Plērōma* is the purpose for creation and the full truth of redemption.

If the End is in the Beginning and the Beginning is in the End (cf. Rev. 1:8; Col. 1:17), how can anything created perfectly in the beginning not come to rest perfectly in the end (*Plērōma*)?

---

[137] See above, n. 2.

God always begins with the End in mind (cf. 1 Pt. 1:20). It is only our lack of an eschatological imagination that fails to grasp the purpose of creation and its perfection in the *Plērōma*.

Our inherent desire for, and ineluctable orientation towards, God is a proleptic participation in the final *Plērōma*. The kingdom of God is already present for those who apprehend their divine humanity in Christ (cf. Jn. 10:34).

It is ontologically impossible for our insatiable desire for God to be stymied by the misuse of our freedom. Finite obstreperousness is no match for the abyss of God's Divine Mercy.

Our God-desired destiny is to be as 'gods in God'[138] (cf. Ps. 82:6; Jn. 10:34; 2 Pt. 1:4) . Our predestined place in God's *Plērōma* is our spiritual pedigree (cf. Eph. 1:4).

Our encounter with the risen Christ deconstructs and recreates our perceptions of God (cf. Php.3:8). Exposure to God's *Plērōma* reveals our limited concepts of God, sin, and death to be 'so much rubbish' (cf. Php. 3:8).

---

[138] See above, n. 30.

What if the Big Bang is a function of the *Plērōma* and not vice versa? What if Christ is the *Omega* before he is the *Alpha*? Wouldn't we need to read Scripture backwards?[139]

What if the cosmic Christ - the Christ of the *Plērōma* - comes *before* the incarnate Christ? What if it is primarily for the sake of his *Plērōma,* not his Passion, that Christ was begotten, conceived, born, suffered, died, rose and ascended?

Only the Holy Spirit can open our hearts to the *Totus Christus* of God's *Plērōma.* We need God's *Sophia* to grasp the *Plērōma* as Christ 'come to full stature' (cf. Eph. 4:13).

The final source of Christian joy is the fact that creation and history are *already* bathed in eschatological glory. Christ is the *Omega Point* of God's begetting Love. Every present moment is a joy-filled anticipation of God's final *Plērōma.*

'Behold, I make all things new!' (cf. Rev. 21:5).

---

[139] For an introduction to an anagogical hermeneutic, see above, n. 116.

GLOSSARY

Apokatastasis – Greek term referring to 'restoration'. In colloquial use, *Apokatastasis* refers to 'universal salvation'. Etymologically derived from *apo* ('back again'), *kathistemi* ('constitute, set down'), and *stasis*, meaning a state, a mode of stability, thus 'return to a former state'. As the 'restoration of all things' *Apokatastasis* is picked up and used among certain Patristic Era theologians in a speculative manner regarding God's eschatological intentions for all creation, including perhaps that which was 'lost' through the Fall.

Acedia - a Greek term meaning 'negligence'. It also connotes apathy and inactivity in the practice of virtue, i.e., spiritual sloth.

Anagogy – Greek, meaning 'to lift up' or 'elevate'. Since the time of Origin, to read Scripture in an anagogical manner is to perceive the *eschatological significance* in an image or passage under consideration. In this sense, anagogical interpretation of Scripture emphasizes the ascendant, deifying dimension of Christian doctrine and experience.

Deification – See *Theosis*.

Diastasis – Greek word used medically to refer to the separation of membranes, but in theology is used to identify and describe the 'infinite qualitative difference' between the self-revealing God and all creaturely attempts to grasp the knowledge of God.

Entelechy - Greek term meaning the vital principle that guides the development and functioning of an organism or other system or organization.

Eschatos/Eschatology – Greek words meaning (1) 'last things' and (2) 'study of last things'. Catechetical enumeration of last things is generally reduced to the 'Four Last Things' of death, judgment, heaven and hell, but more comprehensively eschatology encompasses the Biblical understanding of time, history, and the drive from Creation to the Kingdom of God. The 'now' and 'not yet' presence of the Kingdom presently in the Church is the central subject of Christian eschatology.

Ex nihilo – Latin phrase meaning 'out of nothing' and used in reference to God creating all things freely and gratuitously, without any dependence upon pre-existing matter or from some form of necessity. The doctrine of *creatio ex nihilo* maintains God's transcendence from and freedom toward all that otherwise exists, setting up for a relationship completely predicated upon grace.

Gelassenheit is a German word with multiple meanings: relinquishment, surrender, abandonment, submission, detachment, letting-go, allowing, acquiescence, releasement, etc.

Gnomic – Greek word meaning 'thought' or 'judgment', used in St Maximus in relation to volition; the 'deliberative' will in the sense of having to chose among competing options.

Kerygma – Greek word meaning message or announcement. It is used in the New Testament to refer to the act of preaching, and in time was used to refer to the preached message about salvation.

Kenosis – Greek word used by St Paul to describe the 'self-emptying' of the Son of God in His Incarnation (Philippians 2:7). Such 'self-emptying' or self-donation is perceived as the reciprocal regard each of the Persons of the Trinity pays to each other, can be seen in the Spirit's self-emptying presence in Christ's Body, and becomes a chief aspect of the basic Christian posture toward others.

Kintsugi is the Japanese art of repairing broken pottery by mending the areas of breakage with lacquer dusted or mixed with powdered gold, silver or platinum.

Logos/logoi – Greek term with a wide range of meaning (given here in both singular and plural forms). The root of the English term 'logic' and of the suffix indicating categories of knowledge and study (biology, sociology, etc), logos was employed in the ancient world to describe the rationality informing the existence of all things. The plural logoi was used by Greek-speaking theologians to indicate the inner principle, essence, or intentionality behind all things, which in turn explains their natural participation or fellowship with the Logos, who in Scripture is identified as none other than the Son of God Himself, the Father's agent of creation.

Manichaeism - an elaborate dualistic cosmology, first formulated in the 3rd century CE by the Parthian prophet, Mani (216–274 CE), describing the struggle between a good, spiritual world of light, and an evil, material world of darkness. *Manichaeism* imputes to darkness a power substantially equal and opposite to that of divine Light.

Perichoresis – Greek word meaning "to dance around," and adopted in Christian theology to describe the interpenetrating presence of each Person of the Trinity within each other. The word is useful in giving articulation to the dynamic, mutually-indwelling character of the relations within the divine Trinity, which can then provide insight into the mutual-indwelling character of the relation between Jesus and His people; see John 14: 11; 20; 23.

Pericope - Greek term meaning 'a cutting out'. In Scripture a *pericope* is a set of verses that forms one coherent unit or thought, suitable for public reading from a text, now usually of sacred scripture.

Plērōma – Greek word translated 'fullness', or 'totality'. In Scripture (cf. Jn. 1:12-14; Eph. 1:22-23; Col. 1:19; 2:9-10), it refers to the fullness of God in Christ and the recapitulation and redemption of all things in Christ.

Prolepsis/Proleptic – A technical term used to describe the future-oriented character of Christian identity. It is a term associated with eschatology. Derived from Greek, the word basically means 'anticipation'. A Christian lives his or her life proleptically in the sense that they no longer define themselves in terms of who they used to be or even what they appear to be in the present, but what they will be when the Son of God is disclosed at the End of Time. The classic Biblical expression is 1 John 3:2-3, 'Beloved, we are God's children now; it does not yet appear what we shall be, but we know that when he appears we shall be like him, for we shall see him as he is'.

Protology refers to the study of the origin of things. In theology, *protology* refers to God's act of creation and fundamental purpose for humanity.

Totus Christus – Latin phrase meaning the 'whole Christ', and generally used in reference to the relationship between the Son of God and His Body, the Church, which together, bound in spiritual unity, sacramental presence and ordained ministry constitute the Whole Christ. Rooted in the trinitarian perception that even the Divine Persons are complete only in relation with each other (see *perichoresis*), the doctrine of *Totus Christus* maintains that Jesus is complete only in relationship with His Body, the people he has won to Himself.

Telos – Greek word meaning 'goal' or 'end' toward which something aims and the root of the philosophical term teleology, the study of the fulfillment or purpose of things.

Theosis – Greek term used to express the deification or divinization of human beings. To be deified or divinized is to be so penetrated with the divine as to grow into connaturality with divinity, and so enjoy fellowship with God's nature (see 2 Peter 1:4). While always remaining human, salvation introduces a process of complete transformation which Patristic theologians (particularly of the Greek-speaking Church) describe in a variety of ways, Theosis being chief among them.

Tropos (Greek: τροπη) means 'the way in which' or the 'manner with which' one thing is related to (or oriented towards) another.

Univocal/univocity – From the Latin meaning 'one voice', it refers to a term or meaning that is applied to different things equally. In theology, *univocal* is not set against *equivocal* but placed within *analogy*; words about creation can be used in relation to God in analogous ways, not direct, univocal ways.

Ur-kenosis – In German, the prefix *ur* indicates an original or earliest form of something. Ur-kenosis, then, means the original or first instance of 'self-emptying'.

BIBLIOGRAPHY

Alison, James. 2010. *Raising Abel: The Recovery of the Eschatological Imagination.* SPCK Publishing.

Anselm, St. *Proslogion.* University of Notre Dame Press.

Aquinas, St. Thomas. 2014. *Summa Theologica.* Catholic Way Publishing.

Ark, The Open. 2024. *'Apokatastasis: Part II - on Theophanism'.* May 1, 2024. https://theopenark.substack.com/p/apokatastasis-part-ii.

Athanasius St.. 2013. *On the Incarnation: De Incarnatione Verbi Dei.* Bottom of the Hill Publishing.

Augustine, St.. 2006. *Confessions.* Westminster John Knox.

Balthasar, Hans Urs von. 1994. *Theo-Drama Theological Dramatic Theory. Volume IV, The Action.* Ignatius Press.

_____. 2015. *Theo-Drama: Theological Dramatic Theory / Volume V, The Last Act.* Ignatius Press.

Behr, John. 2006. *The Mystery of Christ : Life in Death.* St. Vladimir SeminaryPress.

Bettelheim, Bruno. 1988. *A Good Enough Parent: A Book on Child-Rearing.* Vintage Books.

Burrell, David B. 1995. *Freedom and Creation in the Abrahamic Traditions.* University of Notre Dame Press.

_____. 2010. *Creation and the God of Abraham.* Cambridge University Press.

Cavey, Bruxy. 2020. *The End of Religion.* Menno Media, Inc.

Cloud of Unknowing, The. 2001. Penguin Books.

Davison, Andrew. 2019. *Participation in God : A Study in Christian Doctrine and Metaphysics.* Cambridge University Press.

Dunn, James D. G. 2008. *The Theology of Paul the Apostle.* Eerdmanns Publishing Company.

Eckhart, Meister. 2014. *Meister Eckhart's Sermons.* Wyatt North Publishing, LLC.

Eliot, T S. 2014. *Four Quartets.* Harper Collins.

Fagerberg, David W. 2022. *Theologia Prima.* LiturgyTraining Publications.

Finlan, Stephen, and Vladimir Kharlamov. 2010. *Theosis.* ISD LLC.

Girard, René. 1989. *The Scapegoat.* Johns Hopkins University Press.

_____. 2002. *Things Hidden since the Foundation of the World.* Stanford University Press.

_____. 1977. *Violence and the Sacred.* Johns Hopkins University Press.

Hamerton-Kelly, Robert. 1994. *The Gospel and the Sacred: Poetics of Violence in Mark.* Augsburg Fortress Publishing.

Hart, David Bentley. 2019. *That All Shall Be Saved : Heaven, Hell, and Universal Salvation.* Yale University Press.

_____. *You Are Gods: On Nature and Supernature.* University of Notre Dame Press.

_____. 2023. *The New Testament: A Translation.* Yale University Press.

_____. 2022. *Tradition and Apocalypse: An Essay on the Future of Christian Belief.* Baker Academic.

Hays, Richard B. 2016. *Reading Backwards: Figural Christology and the Fourfold Gospel Witness.* Baylor University Press.

Irenaeus, St. 2016. *Against Heresies.* Aeterna Press.

Jersak, Brad. 2022. *Out of the Embers: Faith after the Great Deconstruction.* Whitaker House.

Johnathan at Limbo. 2022. *Lecture I: Introduction to Mimetic Theory | René Girard's Mimetic Theory.* YouTube. https://www.youtube.com/watch?v=5Qu6vBebwwg.

John of the Cross, St.. 1991. *The Collected Works of St. John of the Cross.* Institute Of Carmelite Studies.

Julian, Of Norwich. 2019. *Revelations of Divine Love.* Ixia Press.

Nikos Kazantzakis. 2001. *Report to Greco.* Faber.

Kimel, Alvin F. 2022. *Destined for Joy: The Gospel of Universal Salvation.* (Independently Published).

Kharlamov, Vladimir. 2012. *Theosis: Deification in Christian Theology, Volume II.* ISD LLC.

Krill, Philip. 2021. *Gelassenheit: Day-By-Day with Meister Eckhart.* AuthorHouse.

_____. 2024. *Divine Kenosis: Day-By-Day with Hans Urs von Balthasar.* AuthorHouse.

_____. 2017. *Deified Vision: Towards an Anagogical Catholicism.* Lulu.com.

MacDonald, George. 2015. *Consuming Fire : The Inexorable Power of God's Love: A Devotional Version of Unspoken Sermons.* Createspace Independent Publishing Platform.

Maximus, Confessor St.. 2014. *On Difficulties in the Church Fathers: The Ambigua.* Harvard University Press.

Merton, Thomas. 2009. *Conjectures of a Guilty Bystander.* Image Books/Doubleday.

Muggeridge, Malcolm. 1972. *Chronicles of Wasted Time: An Autobiography.* Gateway Books.

Nouwen, Henri. 2006. *With Open Hands.* Ave Maria Press.

Penna, Romano. 1996. Paul the Apostle: Wisdom and Folly of the Cross. Michael Glazier Books.

Rahner, Karl. 2001. *The Trinity.* Burns And Oates.

Ratzinger, Joseph. 2014. *Gospel, Catechesis, Catechism: Sidelights on the Catechism of the Catholic Church.* Ignatius Press.

Reitan, Eric. 2021. *'Is Hard-Heartedness a Good Argument for an Everlasting Hell?'* September 30, 2021. https://www.youtube.com/watch?v=v2SFrnBuO5Q&t=634s.

Russell, Norman. 2005. *The Doctrine of Deification in the Greek Patristic Tradition.* OUP Oxford.

Sanders, Fred. 2005. *The Image of the Immanent Trinity: Rahner's Rule and the Theological Interpretation of Scripture.* Peter Lang.

Sayers, Dorothy L. 2023. *The Mind of the Maker.* Alien Ebooks.

Schweitzer, Albert. 1998. *The Mysticism of Paul the Apostle.* Johns Hopkins University Press.

Soars, Daniel. 2023. The World and God Are Not-Two: *A Hindu-Christian Conversation.* Fordham University Press.

Speyr, Adrienne Von . 1985. *The World of Prayer.* Ignatius Press.

_____. 1993. *The Gospel of John, Volumes I-IV.* Ignatius Press.

_____. 2004. *The Boundless God.* Ignatius Press.

Sutton, Matthew Lewis . 2014. *Heaven Opens: The trinitarian Mysticism of Adrienne von Speyr.* Augsburg Fortress Publishers.

Szarmach, Paul E. 1985. *Introduction to the Medieval Mystics of Europe.* State University of New York Press.

Teresa of Avila, St.. 2010. *The Interior Castle.* Washington, Dc: Ics Publications.

Thunberg, Lars. 1995. *Microcosm and Mediator: The Theological Anthropology of Maximus the Confessor.* Open Court Publishing Company.

Wink, Walter. 1999. *'The Myth of Redemption Violence'*. https://ww2.goshen.edu/~joannab/women/wink99.pdf.

Wood, Jordan Daniel . 2022. *The Whole Mystery of Christ: Creation as Incarnation in Maximus the Confessor.* University of Notre Dame Press.

'You Are Not a Human Being Having a Spiritual Experience. You Are a Spiritual Being Having a Human Experience'. Quote Investigator. June 20, 2019. http://quoteinvestigator. com/2019/06/20/spiritual.

Zizioulas, John D. 2004. *Being as Communion.* Darton Longman & Todd.

_____. 2010. *Communion and Otherness: Further Studies in Personhood and the Church.* Bloomsbury Publishing.